W9-ARJ-132

PINOT, PASTA, *And* PARTIES

DEE DEE And PAUL SORVINO
PINOT, PASTA, And PARTIES

Photography by
VINCENT REMINI

CENTER
STREET®

NEW YORK   NASHVILLE

Center Street
Hachette Book Group
1290 Avenue of the Americas, New York, NY 10104
centerstreet.com
twitter.com/centerstreet

First Edition: April 2017

Center Street is a division of Hachette Book Group, Inc. The Center Street name and logo are trademarks of Hachette Book Group, Inc.

The publisher is not responsible for websites (or their content) that are not owned by the publisher.

The Hachette Speakers Bureau provides a wide range of authors for speaking events. To find out more, go to www.HachetteSpeakersBureau.com or call (866) 376-6591.

Print book interior design by Timothy Shaner, NightandDayDesign.biz

Photos on pgs. 6, 8, 9, courtesy of Il Palato Italiano. Photos pgs. 92,144,170,188,189, 210 from the authors' personal collection. All other photos by Vincent Remini.

ISBNs: 978-1-4555-9689-8 (hardcover), 978-1-4555-9688-1 (ebook)

Printed in the United States of America

LSC-W

10   9   8   7   6   5   4   3   2   1

Dedicated to mom Nancy &
mama Marietta

To Italy for Inspiration

To the United States of America—
the best country in the world

Contents

Contents

WE ♥ NY

LA-LA LAND

SING FOR OUR SUPPER

Contents

Contents

9
PATRIOTISM AT PLAY

10
SHINE ON THE RUNWAY OF LIFE

Dee Dee has the bliss gene.
—PAUL SORVINO

When Paul is around, there is always a reason to celebrate. Paul is a warm, wonderful person, who always has the biggest heart in the room.
—DEE DEE SORVINO

Paul is the ultimate Renaissance man. I have heard that description thrown around a lot, but Paul is the real deal. He loves people, places, art, music, and food. Aside from being a great actor, Paul does so many things remarkably well. He sings opera, creates monumental bronze sculptures, paints, plays the piano and guitar, can do a perfect impression of anyone, is an ace at tennis and archery, and is a genius in the kitchen. I am one lucky girl. —DEE DEE SORVINO

It took me a long time to get it right, but I finally have. The first time I saw Dee Dee she was wearing a periwinkle dress. She had a golden aura around her that was astonishing. I said to myself, "That's the woman for me and she is the most extraordinary woman I have ever met." —PAUL SORVINO

Introduction

A Tale in Two Voices

The odds of us ever meeting were slim, because our worlds do not often intersect.

DEE DEE: I was in politics, originally in the Midwest and then in Washington, DC. Paul lived in Los Angeles, where he had a wonderful acting career. As unlikely as it may seem, our paths crossed on the set for a TV news show in New York. Paul was appearing on the show late in the afternoon of December 11, 2013. I was scheduled to take my chair right after he was done. I was waiting to go onto the set just as he was leaving.

PAUL: I took one look at Dee Dee, and I was smitten. I arranged through the producer for the three of us to have a drink after the show at Del Frisco's, a restaurant next door to the studio. I successfully maneuvered to sit in the chair next to Dee Dee and surprised myself by doing something very much out of character. I am old-school and a gentleman and have never been forward with women. But I was so overwhelmed by the beautiful woman sitting beside me, I was compelled to act. Without a moment's thought, I put my arm around Dee Dee and then leaned in to kiss her. For me, that was that. After twenty years of being single, I knew I had found a woman with whom I could celebrate life. That evening turned into our first dinner. I had planned to meet friends elsewhere, but we ended up staying at Del Frisco's and invited them to join us there.

DEE DEE: I was not expecting anything to come from the meeting. I had lots of friends in town and was enjoying everything New York had to offer. Truth be told, I didn't like actors. I found them demanding. They were like children and divas expecting to have everything revolve around

them. Besides, I was not a fan of Los Angeles, and Paul lived there full-time.

PAUL: When I got back to Los Angeles, I called Dee Dee often, unaware of a serious communications glitch: When Dee Dee returned my calls, her caller ID appeared on my phone as Private Caller. All of her calls were blocked. Though I didn't understand why she was not getting back to me, I continued to call. I was a man on a mission.

DEE DEE: When Paul came back to town to New York to shoot *Brooklyn Banker*, directed by Federico Castelluccio (aka Furio from *The Sopranos*), he went to see me perform in a political satire called *Electoral Dysfunction*. We went to Sardi's after the show, which was our "official" first date. We had a great time. Paul got me a walk-on role at the very end of *Brooklyn Banker*. In the course of the movie, the character Paul was playing went from being a gangster to a boss. The movie ends with all the guys and many extras showing the new capo respect. I was in that scene looking with deference at the boss like everyone else.

PAUL: Not long after *Brooklyn Banker*, I was working on a movie called *Cold Deck* in Canada and asked Dee Dee to join me. One of the stars of the movie invited us for Canadian Thanksgiving dinner, which falls on our Columbus Day. I was so caught up in the spirit of the celebration that I asked Dee Dee to marry me.

"You ask me sitting down?" she responded.

I got down on one knee and proposed again at the Thanksgiving table. I couldn't wait any longer.

Dee Dee accepted.

DEE DEE: We married a little more than two months later, on December 27, 2014, in what I call "the simplest wedding ever." We had a thirty-second ceremony performed by Judge Matthew Sciarrino, my consigliere from early politics, at the fountain at Lincoln Center. Our witnesses were Paul's oldest friend, Paula, and her partner Riccardo, who had joined us for dinner the night we met, our photographer, and Stacy Blum Sciarrino, the judge's wife. A very tight knit wedding party—the only way to elope. Perfect, just the way we wanted it. Our small wedding party walked across the street to celebrate our marriage at Fiorello's. And we are still celebrating.

In *Pinot, Pasta, and Parties*, we have collected our favorite recipes so that you can effortlessly prepare special food for your family and friends. *Pinot, Pasta, and Parties* features ten party menus—from an intimate dinner to a *Goodfellas* feast, from an abundant buffet to a picnic with an Italian accent. We include more than eighty simple recipes that you can enjoy with your guests.

A sample menu begins each chapter. We loosely followed the courses of a traditional Italian meal:

Aperitivo—small bites served with drinks

Antipasto—appetizer

Primi—pasta course

Secondi—main course

Contorni—side dishes

Insalata—salad (always served after the main course)

Dolce—dessert

We are far from formal and go all out only when the occasion merits it. That being said, we can get

excessive at holidays! But if we are serving a six- or seven-course meal, we keep the portions small.

If you don't want to prepare an all-out feast, you can pick and choose from the menus rather than serve every course listed. And though some menus, namely Made in America and Nice Guy Meets Pundit, are designed to be buffets, you can select one or more dishes from those menus for a simple meal for two. Feel free to mix and match these recipes to create a meal that fits your tastes and needs. In every chapter we've added "alternative" recipes for mixing and matching.

We enjoy treating our guests to a great spread. We like to serve them the traditional food they have come to love and expect at our table and to surprise them with new twists on the classics. *Pinot, Pasta, and Parties* provides you with a culinary "playlist" for creating party food guaranteed to delight your friends and family.

BUON APPETITO!

ITALIAN THROUGH AND THROUGH
From Meatballs to Marinara

Roman Days and Italian Knights

DEE DEE: We honeymooned in Rome. It was *perfetto*! I could just feel the history. The Pantheon is one of my favorite buildings in that magnificent city. It has a magical energy that fills me with awe. I've read that when Michelangelo first saw the Pantheon, he said the building was of "angelic and not human design." Originally a pagan temple that had been converted into a Christian church, the Pantheon was 1350 years old when Michelangelo made that observation. The Pantheon is as majestic today, more than 500 years later. Its giant dome, which has a hole on top—an eye, open to the sky—remains the largest in the world.

PAUL: Our honeymoon in Rome was an incredibly beautiful week. Walking the streets of Rome, we were surrounded by art. From masterwork sculptures and paintings in the churches to breathtaking fountains in the piazzas, from modern Italian design in fashion and furniture to stunning blown glass and ceramics, just about everywhere we looked we experienced beauty.

DEE DEE: Paul is at home in Italy, which feeds his aesthetic sense. His Italian heritage is at the root of who he is. He could easily live in Italy. He knows the customs and culinary traditions of every region of the country. The recipes in *Pinot, Pasta, and Parties* capture his deep appreciation of Italian cuisine.

PAUL: Though I was born in the United States, there is something about being Italian that resonates strongly with me. For my charitable work, I was made a Knight of the Great Cross in the Order of the Carinzia, founded by St. George for the protection of the Pope. When the Italians did a background check before making me "Sir Paul," they discovered that my family was noble and had a very long history in and around the city of Naples. I knew my father had been born there, and Neapolitan was the dialect I heard most as a child. I discovered that my family has a coat of arms that dates back to 1150. Despite my aristocratic background in Italy, I still have to come up with cab fare when I'm in New York. So much for nobility!

I consider Italy the font of civilization as we know it today. The Italian Renaissance brought about a richness of intellectual and artistic contributions

> "Paul is at home in Italy, which feeds his aesthetic sense. His Italian heritage is at the root of who he is."
>
> —DEE DEE

that have shaped our culture. Aside from art and music, Italians have affected people in more ways than can be measured. Alessandro Volta discovered the principle that powers the electric battery. Antonio Meucci, an Italian immigrant, invented the first working model of a telephone in 1849, but Alexander Graham Bell got the patent in 1876, although Meucci was there first. And let's not forget Guglielmo Marconi, who developed and demonstrated the first successful long-distance wireless telegraph and broadcast the first transatlantic radio signal in 1901, winning a Nobel Prize in 1909 for his work. The parachute, the machine gun, and the helicopter were all invented by Italians. I am proud to be of Italian descent.

DEE DEE: Paul is saving the best for last—Italian food. To his way of thinking, Italian cuisine is the finest in the world, whether prepared in Italy or just in an Italian manner. Classic Italian cooking is simple and depends on the freshness of the ingredients.

I love to watch Paul work in the kitchen. He really can slice a clove of garlic with a razor blade like Big Paulie in *Goodfellas*! I have learned a lot from Paul about the Italian culture and love for food and drink.

PAUL: I have such great childhood memories of Sunday dinners with my extended family—aunts, uncles, and cousins. I loved sitting around the table eating delicious food and talking about things that were important to us. I wish more of that happened today. Bringing friends and family together for a meal is a joyful ritual. It beats staring at a screen.

I learned to cook mostly from my mother. By the time I was twelve, I was turning out meals for my brothers during the week. I'm comfortable in the kitchen. Cooking is therapy for me. Now that I have Dee Dee to help me, preparing a feast is even more of a joy.

Some of my favorite dishes have been made the same way for centuries, and coming up with new combinations of traditional ingredients is a pleasure for me. I channel my creative energy into so many areas, but preparing delicious food brings me great satisfaction.

DEE DEE: Much of the entertaining we do is a throwback to Paul's Sunday dinners. Fun cocktails, good wine, hearty food, and lively conversation are what it's all about. We love to gather good friends together to enjoy each other's company and a delightful, relaxed meal. When Paul is cooking, everyone wants to join the party.

We wanted the first menu in the book to focus on some Italian classics. In addition to Paul's famous meatballs, we include recipes for eight classic sauces that you can use with pasta, vegetables, salads, meat, chicken, and fish, plus basic recipes for pizza dough, homemade bread crumbs, and Paul's advice about using olive oil.

Menu

Dee Dee's Special Cocktail:
THE ROMAN

Bite-Size ANTIPASTO
MARINARA Sauce
SPAGHETTI and Meatballs
Caprese SALAD
ITALIAN CHEESECAKE
with Lemon Curd Topping

ALTERNATIVE
BRACIOLE

CLASSIC SAUCES
Filetto di POMODORO
RAGU
PESTO
AMATRICIANA
ARRABBIATA
PUTTANESCA
CREAMY VODKA

OTHER BASICS
Paul's PIZZA DOUGH
Homemade BREAD CRUMBS

Dee Dee's Special Cocktail

THE ROMAN

Serves 1

I wanted to create a drink that would make you feel as if you were sitting at a caffè table at the edge of a glorious piazza enjoying the extravagant fountains on a balmy night in Rome. The ingredients represent classic Italian spirits.

2 ounces limoncello
1½ ounces grappa
½ ounce dry vermouth
2 ounces Prosecco
Fresh rosemary sprigs, for garnish

Fill a cocktail shaker halfway with ice. Add the limoncello, grappa, and vermouth. Shake for 5 seconds. Strain into a champagne coupe or flute. Add the Prosecco. Garnish with sprig of rosemary.

Bite-Size ANTIPASTO
Serves 6 to 8

Antipasto can contain any number of ingredients. Our version uses two types of salami, but you should feel free to use whatever Italian cured meats you prefer. We often use slices of prosciutto and pepperoni. Marinated mushrooms, and varied cheese assortments are also good additions.

What we love about this dish is that it can be made several hours ahead and refrigerated without the fresh basil. Just mix in the basil right before you serve.

8 ounces soppressata, cut into ¼-inch-thick slices and quartered

8 ounces Genoa salami, cut into ¼-inch-thick slices and quartered

8 ounces provolone cheese, cut into bite-size pieces

8 ounces bocconcini (small balls of fresh mozzarella cheese)

1 pint cherry tomatoes, halved

1 (14-ounce) can artichokes, drained and quartered

1 cup sliced pepperoncini, drained, 2 tablespoons juice reserved

1 cup halved Peppadew peppers, drained, 2 tablespoons juice reserved

2 teaspoons red pepper flakes

¼ cup green olives, pitted and coarsely chopped

½ cup Kalamata olives, pitted and coarsely chopped

2 tablespoons extra-virgin olive oil

3 tablespoons red wine vinegar

Freshly ground black pepper

¼ cup shredded fresh basil leaves

In a serving bowl, combine the soppressata, Genoa salami, provolone, bocconcini, cherry tomatoes, artichokes, pepperoncini and their juice, Peppadew peppers and their juice, and red pepper flakes. Toss well.

Mix in the chopped olives and toss again. Drizzle the olive oil over everything, followed by the red wine vinegar and a few grinds of black pepper. Mix in the shredded fresh basil leaves just before serving.

MARINARA Sauce

Makes about 8 cups

Marinara sauce is fundamental to Neapolitan cooking. Rather than opening a jar of sauce, try taking the time to make your marinara from scratch. It's simple and doesn't take all that long. Whether you use canned or fresh tomatoes, homemade marinara sauce has so much flavor that any ready-made sauce will be bland in comparison.

This sauce will keep in an airtight container in the refrigerator for up to a week or in the freezer for up to 6 months. We like to freeze smaller portions in individual containers for later use in recipes that do not require an entire pot of sauce.

2 (28-ounce) cans whole peeled San Marzano tomatoes or 24 Roma tomatoes

¼ cup olive oil

4 garlic cloves, thinly sliced

4 fresh basil leaves

⅛ teaspoon dried oregano

If using canned tomatoes, pour the tomatoes and their juices into a large mixing bowl and use your hands to break up the tomatoes until chunky.

If using fresh tomatoes, cut an X into the bottom of each tomato. Blanch the tomatoes in boiling water for 25 seconds, then transfer with a slotted spoon to a large bowl of ice water. When cool enough to handle, peel off the tomato skins and remove the stems. Then use your hands to break up the tomatoes in a bowl until chunky.

Put oil in a large saucepan, heat over medium heat. Add the sliced garlic and sauté until light brown. Add the tomatoes and their juices, basil, and oregano. Simmer until the oil rises to the top, 30 to 40 minutes.

SPAGHETTI and Meatballs
Serves 4 to 6

I am known for my meatballs, which I learned to make as a boy. I was taught that frying the meatballs helps them retain their juiciness.

8 slices white bread
2 pounds ground beef (80% lean)
4 large eggs, lightly beaten
¾ cup grated Pecorino Romano cheese
4 to 6 garlic cloves, minced
½ cup chopped fresh parsley
½ cup seasoned Italian bread crumbs
½ cup light olive oil
1 pound spaghetti
1 recipe Marinara Sauce (page 14), warmed

Wet the bread with warm water and squeeze until the bread becomes a paste the consistency of mashed potatoes.

In a large mixing bowl, mix the bread, beef, eggs, Pecorino Romano, garlic, and parsley by hand. When the ingredients are well combined, add the seasoned bread crumbs slowly until the mixture holds together. (Use more bread crumbs if necessary.)

Form the mixture into balls 2 inches in diameter.

Heat the olive oil in a large skillet over medium heat. Add the meatballs in a single layer. Cook, turning occasionally, until the meatballs are cooked through and evenly browned, about 10 to 15 minutes.

Meanwhile, put a large pot of salted water on the stove to boil. Cook the spaghetti according to the package instructions until al dente, then drain.

Transfer the spaghetti to a large serving dish and top with the meatballs and sauce.

Caprese SALAD

Serves 6 to 8

This salad is best made when tomatoes are in season. I like to use red beefsteak tomatoes because they are so colorful, but any ripe tomato will be delicious. Use the moistest fresh mozzarella you can find.

6 ripe tomatoes, sliced
1 (1-pound) ball fresh buffalo mozzarella, sliced
Sliced red onion (optional)
Fresh basil leaves, some whole and some chopped
Extra-virgin olive oil
Sea salt
Freshly ground black pepper
Chopped yellow bell pepper (optional)

Arrange the tomatoes, mozzarella, onion, and whole basil leaves on a platter or build individual towers. Drizzle with olive oil, season with salt and pepper, and scatter the chopped basil and yellow peppers over the top.

ITALIAN CHEESECAKE with Lemon Curd Topping
Serves 8

This is a refreshing dessert with a light, airy texture and a bold flavor. You can make it a day in advance to get dessert out of the way. Our guests always ask for the recipe for this cheesecake.

FOR THE CHEESECAKE:

8 ounces crushed graham crackers or vanilla wafers

6 tablespoons unsalted butter, melted, plus more at room temperature to grease the pan

1 (32-ounce) container whole-milk ricotta cheese

1 cup sugar

¼ cup all-purpose flour

5 large eggs

1 teaspoon vanilla extract

Grated zest of 1 lemon

FOR THE LEMON CURD TOPPING:

½ cup fresh lemon juice

Grated zest of 1 lemon

¾ cup sugar

3 large eggs

6 tablespoons unsalted butter

Confectioners' sugar, for dusting

Preheat the oven to 350°F.

Grease the bottom and sides of a 9-inch springform pan with a little butter.

In a bowl, mix the cookie crumbs and melted butter. Press the crumb mixture into the bottom of the prepared pan. This crust does not need to be baked.

In the bowl of an electric mixer, beat the ricotta, sugar, and flour on low speed. Add the eggs one at a time and mix until smooth. Add the vanilla and lemon zest and mix until combined.

Pour the cheesecake mixture over the crust and bake until the top of the cheesecake is golden and the center still has some wobble, 1 to 1½ hours.

Let the cake cool on the counter or on a rack before releasing the springform. Before opening the springform, gently loosen the cake all the way around with a butter knife.

Meanwhile, to make the topping, whisk together the lemon juice, lemon zest, sugar, and eggs in a small saucepan. Warm the mixture over low heat, stirring continually, until the curd has thickened, 5 to 7 minutes.

Take the saucepan off the heat and whisk in the butter. Pour the lemon curd into a bowl, cover with plastic wrap, and refrigerate for 1 hour.

Spread the lemon curd over the cooled cheesecake as if you are frosting a cake. Refrigerate the cheesecake until it is cold, or until you can't wait any longer to eat it! Before serving, dust lightly with confectioners' sugar.

BRACIOLE

Serves 4 to 6

Braciole is simply meat rolled around stuffing. It can be served as a rolled roast with sauce on the side or as individual steak rolls cooked in marinara sauce with meatballs and sausage with pasta for Sunday dinner. Be creative when you make braciole. You can put anything in the stuffing—chopped hardboiled eggs, prosciutto, salami, onion, pine nuts, raisins, or any kind of Italian cheese. Braciole can also be made with chicken, pork, or veal.

6 slices beef top round (about 1½ pounds), pounded to a thickness of ¼ inch
1¼ teaspoons sea salt, divided
¾ teaspoon freshly ground black pepper, divided
½ cup seasoned Italian bread crumbs
1 large egg, lightly beaten

2 tablespoons minced garlic
⅔ cup chopped fresh flat-leaf parsley
1 cup grated Parmesan cheese
1 cup grated provolone cheese
3 tablespoons olive oil, divided
¾ cup water

Lay out the beef slices flat on a work surface and season with ¾ teaspoon of the salt and ½ teaspoon of the pepper.

In a medium bowl, mix the seasoned bread crumbs, egg, garlic, parsley, Parmesan, provolone, and 1 tablespoon of the olive oil. Scoop ½ cup of the bread crumb mixture onto each piece of beef and spread it along the edge of the short end closest to you.

Roll up the beef around the stuffing and tie it in a few places with butcher's twine to secure. Repeat with the remaining rolls. Season the braciole with the remaining ½ teaspoon salt and ¼ teaspoon pepper.

In a large skillet, heat 1 tablespoon of olive oil over medium-high heat. Working in batches and adding the remaining tablespoon of oil as needed, cook the braciole, turning occasionally, until browned on all sides, about 8 minutes per batch.

Transfer the rolls to a roasting pan as they are done. Pour the water into the pan and roast for 45 minutes. Slice the braciole and serve. (Alternatively, you can add the browned braciole to a pot of simmering Marinara Sauce [page 14] and simmer for 2 hours.)

CLASSIC SAUCES

Nothing goes together better than sauce and pasta—it's a perfect marriage. Whether you're serving a pasta course, a pasta side dish for a simpler meal, or a big bowl of pasta with crusty bread and a salad for a main course, you can select from the recipes for classic sauces we have collected here anytime you want to a change from basic Marinara Sauce (page 14).

POMODORO

To make this type of tomato sauce, follow the Marinara Sauce recipe (page 14), but substitute 1 medium sliced onion for the sliced garlic. (Neapolitans never mix onion and garlic in a sauce, because their flavors cancel each other out.) Sauté the onion until caramelized. Some people make this sauce with larger chunks of tomatoes for a thicker consistency.

Paul on Using the Right Olive Oil

Though people seem to use extra-virgin olive oil for everything now, I consider it a finishing oil and never cook with it. Extra-virgin olive oil is the most flavorful, but it becomes bitter when you cook it. It is best drizzled on vegetables or salads, stirred into soups just before eating, or as a dipping sauce. Good-quality olive oil does the job for cooking. I sometimes use light olive oil for frying and sautéing, depending on the recipe.

RAGU

Serves 12

Ragu is a meat-based tomato sauce. It is the traditional Italian Sunday dinner sauce. This sauce will keep in an airtight container in the refrigerator for up to a week or in the freezer for up to 6 months.

5 (28-ounce) cans whole peeled San Marzano tomatoes or 36 Roma tomatoes
½ cup olive oil
5 ounces stewing beef
5 ounces stewing veal
½ rack pork ribs
1 medium onion, diced
6 fresh basil leaves
1 teaspoon sea salt

If using canned tomatoes, pour the tomatoes and their juices into a large mixing bowl and use your hands to break up the tomatoes until chunky.

If using fresh tomatoes, cut an X into the bottom of each tomato. Blanch the tomatoes in boiling water for 25 seconds, then transfer with a slotted spoon to a large bowl of ice water. When cool enough to handle, peel off the tomato skins and remove the stems. Then use your hands to break up the tomatoes in a bowl until chunky.

In a large saucepan, warm the olive oil over medium heat. Brown the meat and ribs in a single layer, turning for an even sear. Transfer the meat to a bowl. Add the onion to the oil remaining in the pan and sauté until brown. Return the meat to the saucepan.

Add the tomatoes and their juices, basil, and salt. Simmer on low heat for 4 hours, stirring occasionally. The meat will break up during the cooking time.

PESTO

Serves 4 to 6

Classic pesto is a summery sauce, because fresh basil is in season then. It takes no time to whip up this versatile sauce in a food processor. There is no end to what you can do with pesto sauce—we use it on pasta, eggs, vegetables, meat, and fish, in salad dressings, dips, and soups, and as a sandwich spread.

Pesto will keep in an airtight container in the refrigerator for up to a week. It also freezes well, so you can make a big batch at the end of basil season in the fall to save for the winter. We like to freeze the pesto in ice cube trays, then transfer the frozen pesto cubes to plastic freezer bags for up to 6 months. That way, we can defrost the cubes in the quantities we need.

2 cups fresh basil leaves
2 garlic cloves, minced
½ cup pine nuts
1¼ cups extra-virgin olive oil
½ cup grated Parmesan cheese
½ cup grated Pecorino Romano cheese
¾ teaspoon sea salt

Combine the basil, garlic, and pine nuts in a food processor and process for 15 seconds.

With the processor running, pour 1 cup of the olive oil through the feed tube in a steady stream, then gradually add the cheeses, followed by the remaining oil. Season the pesto with the salt.

AMATRICIANA

Serves 6 to 8

This classic sauce for pasta originated in Amatrice, a town an hour east of Rome. In Italy, the sauce is made with guanciale, which is Italian salt-cured pork jowl. You can find guanciale in gourmet stores, but unsliced pancetta or prosciutto works just as well.

2 (28-ounce) cans whole peeled San Marzano tomatoes

3 tablespoons olive oil

8 ounces guanciale, pancetta, or prosciutto, cut into ½-inch chunks

1 red onion, thinly sliced

½ teaspoon red pepper flakes

Sea salt

Freshly ground black pepper

Pour the tomatoes and their juices into a large mixing bowl and use your hands to break up the tomatoes until chunky.

Heat the olive oil in a large skillet over low heat. Add the meat and cook, turning occasionally, about 15 minutes. Use a slotted spoon to transfer the meat to a plate.

Add the onion to the oil remaining in the pan and sauté for 5 minutes. Add the tomatoes and their juices. Add the red pepper flakes and season with salt and black pepper to taste. Simmer for 20 minutes, stirring occasionally.

Add the meat to the sauce in the skillet and toss to coat.

You can store the sauce in an airtight container in the refrigerator for up to a week or in the freezer for up to 6 months.

ARRABBIATA
Serves 6 to 8

This quick, easy tomato sauce has a real kick. It will liven up any meal, but it's especially great with penne.

2 (28-ounce) cans whole peeled San Marzano tomatoes
2 tablespoons olive oil
2 garlic cloves, minced
1 hot red pepper, halved and seeded
⅛ teaspoon dried oregano
1 teaspoon dried basil or 4 to 5 fresh basil leaves, cut into ribbons
½ teaspoon crushed red pepper flakes
Sea salt

Pour the tomatoes and their juices into a large mixing bowl and use your hands to break up the tomatoes until chunky.

In a skillet, warm the olive oil over medium heat. Add the garlic and sauté until golden. Add the hot red pepper, oregano and dried basil (if using) and cook, stirring constantly, for 1 minute.

Add the tomatoes and their juices. Remove the hot red pepper halves and add the red pepper flakes. Bring the sauce to a boil.

Lower the heat to medium-low, cover, and cook, stirring every 5 minutes, until the oil has separated and shows on the sides of the pan, 20 to 25 minutes. Taste and add salt if needed.

This sauce will keep in an airtight container in the refrigerator for up to a week or in the freezer for up to 6 months.

Before serving, add the fresh basil (if using).

PUTTANESCA

Serves 6 to 8

This spicy, salty sauce is a mid-twentieth-century creation that originated in Naples. Its name means "in the style of a prostitute." It is said that ladies of the night made this sauce to lure men with its aromas.

What is terrific about this sauce is that it's made from ingredients that are usually on hand in a well-stocked pantry. You never know when you are ready for seduction!

2 (28-ounce) cans whole peeled
  San Marzano tomatoes
¼ cup olive oil
4 garlic cloves, minced
4 anchovy fillets, finely chopped
¼ teaspoon crushed red pepper flakes
1 tablespoon tomato paste
¼ teaspoon sugar
⅛ teaspoon dried oregano
½ cup chopped Kalamata olives
1½ tablespoons capers, drained

Sea salt
Freshly ground black pepper
1 tablespoon chopped fresh flat-leaf parsley
Grated Parmesan cheese, for serving

Pour the tomatoes and their juices into a large mixing bowl and use your hands to break up the tomatoes until chunky.

Heat the oil in a large saucepan over medium heat. Add the garlic, anchovies, and red pepper flakes and cook for 5 minutes. And the tomatoes and their juices.

Stir in the sugar, oregano, olives, and capers. Season with salt and pepper to taste and bring to a boil. Simmer the sauce over low heat, stirring occasionally, until it thickens, about 30 minutes. Season again with salt and pepper.

When serving, add the fresh parsley when tossing the sauce with cooked pasta. Serve with grated Parmesan cheese.

This sauce will keep in an airtight container in the refrigerator for up to a week or in the freezer for up to 6 months.

Creamy VODKA

Serves 6 to 8

There is confusion about the origins of this sweet, salty, comforting sauce, which came into popularity in the United States in the late '70s and early '80s. Some believe that vodka distillers invented the sauce and pushed it on chefs. Others believe Italian-Americans in New York created the sauce. Wherever it came from, creamy vodka sauce with penne, ziti, or fusilli is rich and warming on a winter night.

2 (28-ounce) cans whole peeled San Marzano tomatoes
2 tablespoons olive oil
¼ cup minced shallot
3 garlic cloves, minced
1 tablespoon tomato paste
¼ teaspoon crushed red pepper flakes
⅓ cup vodka
½ cup heavy cream
Sea salt

Pour the tomatoes and their juices into a large mixing bowl and use your hands to break up the tomatoes until chunky.

In a medium saucepan, warm the olive oil over medium heat. Add the shallot and cook until browned, about 5 minutes. Stir in the garlic, tomato paste, and red pepper flakes and cook for 1 minute.

Add the tomatoes and their juices and the vodka. Simmer, stirring occasionally, until the alcohol cooks off, 7 to 10 minutes.

If you prefer a smooth sauce, pour the mixture into a blender or food processor and puree. Return the sauce to the saucepan.

Add the heavy cream and cook over medium heat until warmed through, 2 to 3 minutes. Season with salt to taste.

This sauce can be stored in an airtight container in the refrigerator for up to a week or in the freezer for up to 6 months.

Paul's PIZZA DOUGH

Other Basics

Makes 2 medium crusts

We love homemade pizza! Making your own pizza crust is part of the fun. We sometimes have small "Make Your Own Pizza" parties. We set out bowls of sliced vegetables, pepperoni, salami, prosciutto, meatballs, and a selection of cheeses, sauces, and plenty of pizza dough ready for our guests to make personal pies. Endless combinations of toppings are possible! If the oven gets too crowded, we cook the pizza outside on the grill.

¾ cup warm water

1 packet active dry yeast

3 tablespoons olive oil

1 teaspoon sugar

¾ teaspoon sea salt

1 cup all-purpose flour

1 cup bread flour

In a stand mixer fitted with the paddle attachment, combine the warm water and yeast. Allow the mixture to sit for 5 minutes, then add the oil, sugar, and salt.

Start the mixer on low and carefully add the flours. Mix on low to medium for 30 to 60 seconds to combine fully.

Switch out the paddle attachment for the dough hook. Allow the dough hook to work the dough for 4 to 5 minutes.

Transfer the dough to a lightly floured airtight container. Chill in the refrigerator for 2 hours before using. Use the dough within 24 hours. (See pizza recipes on pages 64, 79, 103, and 215.)

Homemade BREAD CRUMBS

Homemade bread crumbs have more flavor and better texture than those you buy at the grocery store. And it's a great use for leftover bread. The bread crumbs will keep in an airtight container in the refrigerator for up to 1 month or in the freezer for up to 3 months.

Bread slices, fresh or slightly stale

Preheat the oven to 350°F.

Lay out the bread slices in a single layer on a baking sheet and toast in the oven until golden, about 10 minutes. Set aside to cool, then tear into chunks.

Put the bread chunks in small batches in a food processor and pulse until the bread crumbs are the size you want.

Feel free to customize your bread crumbs with fresh or dried herbs, grated cheese, crushed red pepper flakes, minced garlic, or grated lemon zest.

MADE IN AMERICA

2

From California to the New York Island

DEE DEE: We live in the best country in the world! Paul and I are patriots. We make a point of celebrating Independence Day and Veterans Day by wearing red, white, and blue. Paul loves Italy with all his heart, but he is 100 percent American. He proudly served his country in the military.

I am a girl born in Kentucky and raised across the Ohio river in the America's heartland, Indiana. My people came from Scotland. Many Scots-Irish made the migration to Appalachia around the time of the American Revolution. My family was of the Napier clan, known to be warriors. Many Scots fought for our independence from England. Scot pioneers such as Daniel Boone made their mark on our young country.

PAUL: I feel lucky to have been born in America. The despair and difficulty of other civilizations has rarely visited us here. This is the place where dreams can come true. I still believe that if you work hard, success will come your way, even if it's not the success you had imagined.

My grandfather Alfonso Sorvino and his wife, Concetta, had seven daughters and three sons. In Italy, they would have had to provide a dowry for every girl child. Although the family Sorvino was not poor, they did not have the dowries to make good marriages for their seven daughters. Rather than settle for less than excellent marriages for their girls, my grandparents decided to go to America, where dowries were not expected. They boarded a ship to the United States in 1907, and I am so grateful they did.

As a member of the first generation of Sorvinos born in the States, I served in the military for this great country. The history of America moves me. It bears a magnificent hope—the hope of the world. A young country filled with vigor, America is rebellious. At the same time it is warmhearted and generous—the most generous country in history. God bless America.

DEE DEE: We took our first big trip to Los Angeles as newlyweds by train, which I had always planned to do. We wanted to see this great land of ours. Paul is a big guy, so staying in our tiny compartment was a challenge for him. He was a good sport about it.

I packed wine, Champagne, candles, and snacks to add to the romance. We would have a toast as

"The history of America moves me. It bears a magnificent hope—the hope of the world."

—PAUL

"I am the proudest American girl, America first!"

—DEE DEE

the sun went down each night. It was frigid January when we left New York, but as we got closer to California on the southern route, it became sunnier and warmer, which made Paul happy. When we finally made it to the train station in Los Angeles, we decided our journey had been a wonderful way to see the country we loved.

On a later trip, we decided to drive across the country, making stops at points of interest along the way. Paul loves anything cowboy, so he enjoyed our stop at the Big Texan Steak Ranch. If you can put away a seventy-two-ounce steak, you get the steak for free! I bought him a little Texas Ranger badge there that he still has.

PAUL: My childhood love of cowboy stories and songs has never left me. When I read to go to sleep, I'm usually reading a western. I have to confess that we watch a lot of old westerns on TV.

DEE DEE: We made our last cross-country trip in my new car. Since everyone in Los Angeles has a car, Paul wanted to buy me one for my birthday. I could have had any car I wanted, but I didn't want a fancy, foreign car like everyone else in Los Angeles.

When I said, "I want an American-made car, and the most American car is a Ford," he was surprised. He bought me a fully loaded Ford Explorer.

We enjoyed the changes in scenery and weather during our transcontinental drive in my new Ford. Paul loves A&W root beer, so we were always searching for those frosty mugs on the road.

This chapter offers a down-home American picnic with an Italian slant. We love to entertain our guests al fresco in Los Angeles. As homage to cowboys and westerns, we've included Spaghetti Western Mac and Cheese and Paul's outstanding chili.

Menu

Dee Dee's Special Cocktail:
APPALACHIA MAGIC

Chicken PARMIGIANA STICKS
with Marinara Sauce

Spaghetti Western MAC AND CHEESE

Meatball SLIDERS

Paul's Special CHILI

EGGPLANT AND ZUCCHINI Fries with Aioli

POLENTA with Broccoli Sauce

Caesar SALAD

Stars and Stripes FRUIT PIZZA

ALTERNATIVE
SLOPPY GIO

Dee Dee's Special Cocktail
APPALACHIA MAGIC
Serves 1

One impressive fact about my favorite president, George Washington, is that after leaving office he went into the whiskey business and made a ton of money.

We think moonshine must be uniquely American. You never hear about moonshine in France or Germany. With my Kentucky roots, moonshine is definitely in my lexicon and on the menu. When we went out to buy the 'shine, we were informed that it's a hot commodity now, a hip alcohol, on its way to number one.

One sip of my Appalachia Magic will make you break into a chorus of "America the Beautiful" and chants of "USA! USA!"

3 ounces moonshine
2 ounces apple cider
¼ ounce fresh lemon juice
6 dashes cinnamon bitters
1 whole star anise

Fill a cocktail shaker one-quarter of the way with ice. Add the moonshine, apple cider, lemon juice, and bitters. Shake vigorously for 10 seconds. Strain into a mason jar–style rocks glass filled with ice. Garnish with the star anise.

Chicken PARMIGIANA STICKS with Marinara Sauce

Makes 16 sticks

C runchy on the outside with warm, gooey cheese inside, this perfect finger food is a big hit whenever we serve them. You might want to double the recipe. Forget about chicken tenders—kids of all ages love these chicken treats with a surprise inside.

2 tablespoons olive oil

2 pounds ground chicken breast

4 large eggs, lightly beaten, divided

2 garlic cloves, minced

1 tablespoon dried parsley or 3 tablespoons minced fresh flat-leaf parsley

½ teaspoon dried oregano or 3 tablespoons minced fresh oregano

1 teaspoon sea salt

1 teaspoon freshly ground black pepper

1 pound mozzarella cheese, cut into 16 sticks

1 cup all-purpose flour

2 cups seasoned Italian bread crumbs

1 cup grated Parmesan cheese

2 cups Marinara Sauce (page 14), warm, for serving

Preheat the oven to 400°F. Spread the oil on a rimmed baking sheet.

Using your hands, mix the ground chicken, 2 of the beaten eggs, the garlic, parsley, oregano, salt, and pepper in a large bowl.

Mold about ¼ cup of the chicken mixture around each mozzarella stick to enclose it completely.

Put the flour in a shallow baking dish or pie plate. Put the remaining 2 beaten eggs in a small bowl. Mix the seasoned bread crumbs and Parmesan cheese in a shallow bowl. Dredge each chicken stick first in the flour, then in the egg, and finally in the bread crumb mixture and place in a single layer on the oiled baking sheet.

Bake for 15 to 20 minutes, turning to make sure all sides are golden brown. Serve immediately with warmed marinara sauce for dipping.

Spaghetti Western MAC AND CHEESE
Serves 4 to 6

My love of all things cowboy inspired this take on mac and cheese. When we want to go all out, we use wagon wheel pasta to carry on the theme. You can make this dish in advance and reheat it right before serving.

8 ounces ground beef

1 garlic clove, minced

¾ teaspoon ground cumin

½ teaspoon sea salt

Freshly ground black pepper

1 (28-ounce) can crushed tomatoes

4 tablespoons (½ stick) salted butter

2 tablespoons all-purpose flour

2 cups whole milk

¾ cup grated Parmesan cheese

1 pound spaghetti or wagon wheel pasta

1½ cups shredded cheese, such as
     fontina, smoked Gouda, or Jarlsberg

8 ounces fresh mozzarella cheese,
     cut in ¼-inch-thick slices

In a skillet, fry the ground beef over medium heat until browned, about 6 minutes. Drain off the fat. Add the garlic, cumin, sea salt, and pepper to taste. Stir in the tomatoes. Reduce the heat to medium-low and cook, stirring occasionally, until most of the liquid has reduced, 30 to 35 minutes.

Meanwhile, preheat the oven to 350°F.

Put a large pot of salted water on the stove to boil. Cook the pasta for 5 minutes. The pasta should not be cooked completely, because it will continue to cook in the oven. Drain and set aside.

In a medium saucepan, melt the butter over low heat. Whisk in the flour gradually. Raise the heat to medium. Add the milk and whisk continuously for 4 minutes. Lower the heat if the liquid is about to boil. It should thicken and be smooth. Remove the saucepan from the heat. Stir in the Parmesan.

In an 8-inch square nonstick baking pan, layer half of the pasta, meat mixture, cheese sauce, and shredded cheese. Repeat to make another layer of each. Top with the mozzarella slices.

Bake until the cheese is melted and golden brown, 30 to 40 minutes.

Meatball SLIDERS
Makes 10 sliders

*H*ere's my take on the hamburger slider. These are perfect for a crowd—
try them on movie or game night!

1 pound ground beef
1 pound spicy Italian sausage, meat removed from casings
½ cup finely chopped onion
2 tablespoons minced fresh thyme or 2 teaspoons dried thyme
1 tablespoon minced fresh flat-leaf parsley or 1 teaspoon dried parsley
1 large egg, lightly beaten
¼ cup olive oil
1 cup Homemade Bread Crumbs (page 38)
2 teaspoons sea salt
½ teaspoon red pepper flakes
2 cups Marinara Sauce (page 14)
10 brioche slider buns
Shaved Parmesan cheese, for serving

Preheat the oven to 400°F.

In a large bowl, combine the ground beef, sausage, onion, herbs, egg, olive oil, bread crumbs, and salt by hand until well mixed. Let stand for 5 to 10 minutes.

Roll into 10 meatballs about 1½ inches in diameter and put them on a rimmed baking sheet or in a cast iron skillet. Bake until cooked through, 15 to 17 minutes.

Add the red pepper flakes to the marinara sauce and warm in a saucepan over medium-low heat.

When the meatballs are done, place them on the buns, spoon marinara sauce over them, and top with Parmesan shavings.

Paul's Special CHILI

Serves 6 to 8

W*hat makes chili a fun party dish is that we put out bowls of different toppings so that our guests can pick and choose to customize their chili. Whether we enjoy a bowl on our own while we watch TV or make the chili and various toppings the centerpiece of a buffet, this recipe never disappoints and always delivers great flavor.*

¼ cup olive oil

4 garlic cloves, minced

2 (15-ounce) cans red kidney beans, undrained

2 pounds ground beef

1 (16-ounce) can tomato sauce or diced tomatoes, undrained

1 tablespoon ground cumin

¼ teaspoon cayenne pepper

2 to 3 tablespoons chili powder

1 teaspoon sea salt

Freshly ground black pepper

8 ounces penne

Optional toppings: shredded lettuce, shredded Cheddar and/or Monterey Jack cheese,
   sour cream, diced tomatoes, diced bell peppers, diced onions, sliced jalapeño or
   banana peppers, diced avocado, sliced black olives, spicy salsa

In a large saucepan, heat the olive oil over medium high heat. Add the garlic and cook until slightly brown, 3 to 5 minutes. Add the beans straight from the cans—do not drain.

While the beans heat up, fry the ground beef in a skillet over medium heat until browned, about 8 minutes. Add the meat to the bean mixture. Stir in the tomato sauce and spices and cook over low heat, stirring occasionally, for 35 minutes.

Meanwhile, put a large pot of salted water on the stove to boil for the pasta. Cook the pasta until al dente, 10 to 12 minutes. Drain the pasta and mix it into the chili.

Ladle the chili into bowls and serve with a selection of toppings.

EGGPLANT AND ZUCCHINI FRIES with Aioli

Serves 8

Get ready for an Italian take on french fries. A favorite appetizer in Italy, fritto misto *(mixed fry)* is an assortment of bite-size pieces of vegetables that are dipped in batter and deep-fried. I have changed the traditional recipe by broiling the battered vegetables, making misto alla griglia, *or mixed grill. If you want to make fritto misto instead, you can deep-fry the battered vegetables rather than broiling them.*

The eggplant and zucchini "fries" can be served with marinara sauce or ketchup, but we like it with a garlicky mayonnaise known as aioli.

FOR THE AIOLI:

2 garlic cloves, minced

¼ teaspoon coarse sea salt, plus more for seasoning

½ cup mayonnaise

2 tablespoons olive oil

1 tablespoon fresh lemon juice

Freshly ground black pepper

FOR THE FRIES:

2 tablespoons olive oil, divided

1 (1- to 1½-pound) eggplant

3 (1-pound) zucchinis

2 cups Homemade Bread Crumbs (page 38)

¼ cup grated Parmesan cheese

¼ teaspoon each dried oregano, parsley, and basil

½ teaspoon granulated garlic

3 large eggs, lightly beaten

First, make the aioli. Mash the garlic and salt in a small bowl until a paste forms. Whisk in the mayonnaise, oil, and lemon juice. Season with salt and pepper to taste. Refrigerate until ready to serve. (You can make the aioli up to one day ahead of serving.)

Preheat the broiler. Coat a rimmed baking sheet with olive oil.

Cut the eggplant in half lengthwise and then in half crosswise to get four quarters. Cut each quarter into ½-inch-thick strips. Repeat with each zucchini.

In a shallow dish, combine the bread crumbs, Parmesan cheese, dried herbs, and granulated garlic.

Dip the vegetable sticks into the beaten eggs and then coat with the bread crumb mixture. Put the vegetables in a single layer on the baking sheet. Brush a bit of olive oil on the sticks.

Broil for 3 to 4 minutes. Flip the sticks and drizzle with olive oil. Broil until golden brown, 2 to 3 minutes longer. Serve warm, with the aioli for dipping.

POLENTA with Broccoli Sauce

Serves 6 to 8

Polenta is the ultimate comfort food, and pairing it with broccoli makes it hearty as well as healthy. I have found that using instant polenta saves time but does not diminish the texture of the finished dish.

FOR THE BROCCOLI SAUCE:

6 cups water
1 (1½-pound) bunch broccoli
Sea salt
½ cup olive oil
4 garlic cloves, minced
Freshly ground black pepper

FOR THE POLENTA:

6 cups water
2 teaspoons sea salt
2 cups instant polenta
3 tablespoons unsalted butter
½ cup grated Parmesan cheese, plus more for serving
½ teaspoon dried sage
½ teaspoon freshly ground black pepper

First, start the broccoli sauce. In a large saucepan, bring the water to a boil over medium-high heat.

While the water is heating, prepare the broccoli by discarding the stalks that are pale green or very white. Trim the base of the tender stalks and peel the stalks with a paring knife. Cut the stalks into 1-inch pieces and break up the florets into small clusters.

Salt the boiling water, add the broccoli, cover, and cook for 20 minutes.

While the broccoli is cooking, make the polenta. In a large saucepan, bring the water and salt to a boil over high heat. Stir the polenta into the boiling water in a slow, steady stream, whisking constantly. Reduce the heat to medium and continue whisking until the polenta has thickened, about 5 minutes. Remove the

saucepan from the heat and stir in the butter, Parmesan cheese, sage, and pepper. Cover and set aside while you finish the broccoli sauce.

When the broccoli is done, use a slotted spoon to transfer it to a cutting board. Reserve the cooking water. Coarsely chop the broccoli.

Heat the olive oil in a medium skillet over low heat. Add the garlic and sauté until softened, 2 to 3 minutes. Stir in the broccoli and sauté for 5 minutes.

Add 1 cup of the reserved broccoli cooking water, turn up the heat to medium, and bring the liquid to a boil. Then, reduce the heat to medium-low and simmer, adding more of the reserved water, ½ cup at a time, as it evaporates and using a wooden spoon to break down the broccoli into a coarse puree, about 15 minutes. Season with salt and pepper to taste.

Mound the polenta on a serving dish and make a large, shallow indentation in the center with the back of a large spoon. Spoon the broccoli and juices from the skillet into the indentation, letting some of the juices run over the sides of the polenta. Grind some pepper over the broccoli. Serve with additional grated Parmesan on the side.

SLOPPY GIO

Serves 4

Get ready for sloppy Joe's, Italian-style. The Italian ingredients add layers of flavor to this American classic.

2 pounds ground beef (80% lean)

3 cups Marinara Sauce (page 14)

1 teaspoon dried basil

4 ciabatta rolls

Olive oil

8 ounces shredded Italian cheese blend, such as smoked provolone, Pecorino Romano, fontina, Asiago, and/or Parmesan

4 slices fresh mozzarella cheese

In a heavy skillet, fry the beef over medium heat until browned, about 8 minutes. Drain off the fat. Add the marinara sauce and dried basil and cook until the sauce has reduced and thickened, about 35 minutes.

Meanwhile, preheat the broiler.

Slice the rolls and brush with olive oil. Place the rolls on a baking sheet and toast them briefly under the broiler.

Spoon some of the meat mixture onto each bun. Sprinkle with the shredded cheese. Top with a slice of fresh mozzarella and broil again, just until the cheese bubbles and browns.

Caesar SALAD

Serves 6 to 8

This classic salad takes no time to prepare. The dressing makes it delicious, and we like adding cherry tomatoes for color.

2 garlic cloves, minced
2 tablespoons fresh lemon juice
½ teaspoon anchovy paste
1 teaspoon Dijon mustard
Sea salt
¼ cup extra-virgin olive oil
1 head romaine lettuce
Cherry tomatoes
Freshly ground black pepper
Grated Parmesan cheese

Combine the garlic, lemon juice, anchovy paste, mustard, and a pinch of salt in a blender and mix. With the blender running, slowly drizzle in the olive oil and mix until smooth.

Arrange the lettuce leaves and tomatoes on a platter or toss together in a salad bowl. Drizzle with the dressing, add a few grinds of black pepper, and sprinkle the grated Parmesan cheese over the top.

Stars and Stripes FRUIT PIZZA

Serves 10 to 12

This stars and stripes pizza is an inspiration and a reminder of how great our country is. This showpiece dessert is perfect for a picnic or a patriotic holiday like the Fourth of July—and it's easy to make. Using pizza dough or puff pastry sheets is a novel way to go.

¼ cup cornmeal

1 pound mascarpone cheese

½ cup confectioners' sugar

All-purpose flour, for dusting

1 recipe Paul's Pizza Dough (page 36) or 1 sheet frozen puff pastry

1 pint raspberries or strawberries

1 pint blueberries

Preheat the oven to 500°F. Scatter the cornmeal on a rimmed baking sheet to prevent sticking.

Beat together the mascarpone and confectioners' sugar by hand until smooth, then refrigerate until ready to top the pizza.

Dust a work surface well with flour.

If using pizza dough, use a rolling pin and your hands to form the pizza dough into a large rectangle. Transfer the pizza to the prepared baking sheet and bake until the pizza dough is golden, about 15 minutes. Allow the crust to cool completely before adding the toppings.

If using frozen puff pastry, defrost and bake according to the package directions. Cool and cut the pastry in half. You will now have two halves to fill if you want to double the recipe; otherwise, reserve the remaining half for another use.

While the crust is cooling, slice the strawberries lengthwise for the flag's stripes (if using raspberries, they can go on the crust whole).

Spread the mascarpone mixture all over the cooled dough.

Arrange the blueberries in a rectangle in the left corner to represent our fifty states, leaving space between the blueberries so that the mascarpone shows through.

Line up the strawberries or raspberries in stripes separated by a mascarpone stripe to create the flag. This is a wonderful dessert to make with the kids. They love creating the flag!

If not serving immediately, refrigerate the "flag" so the mascarpone does not melt.

WE ♥ NY

Brooklyn Born

How could we not love New York? After all, we met and married in that great city and live there part-time. We believe that New York City has the best energy and the smartest, most creative people in the world. There is a level of excitement in the city that is hard to find anywhere else.

We love to walk all over town and never fail to be amazed at the staggering number of wonderful restaurants, cafés, specialty stores, fashion boutiques, and businesses we pass. Since it's a walking city, people watching is a great entertainment. Talk about a melting pot! We hear every language in the world on the sidewalks of New York.

We love the fast pace, we love the diversity, and we love the food. From Little Italy to Koreatown, from Curry Hill to Restaurant Row in the theater district, food choices are limitless—and so are markets, where you can find any ingredient you can dream of.

PAUL: I was born in Brooklyn, in 1939, an auspicious year—the year of *The Wizard of Oz, Gone with the Wind,* and the New York World's Fair. The Brooklyn I grew up in was a lively place with a culture all its own, the Brooklyn Dodgers being the kingpins. To this day, I find it hard to forgive them for leaving.

Though Brooklyn was a beautiful mix of ethnicities and cultures, I especially admired the Italians with their sometimes rough and tumble but always entertaining qualities. The Neapolitans, my people, had a special kind of joy, a vibrancy I have not seen in most people.

I got a lot from my early years in Brooklyn, most importantly a personality that is ready for just about anything. Nothing much surprises me.

When I was thirteen, I longed to go to the city, as we called it, especially Greenwich Village. In my early twenties, I moved to Manhattan, took voice lessons, and learned my trade as an actor.

"Though Brooklyn was a beautiful mix of ethnicities and cultures, I especially admired the Italians with their sometimes rough and tumble but always entertaining qualities."

—PAUL

DEE DEE: Paul is revered everywhere in New York City—and, really, all over the state. He is recognized everywhere. Everyone wants to say hello to "Big Paulie." We were alarmed one day when two policemen ran after us, they just wanted a picture with uncle Paulie.

The first big party I threw for Paul was at a New York steak house. It was an amazing night. Paul's co-star from *Law & Order,* Chris Noth (aka Mr. Big from *Sex and the City*), was there to celebrate. Supermodel Carol Alt, boxer Evander Holyfield, and Governor Andrew Cuomo all came to honor Paul, along with family and many other friends.

The governor made a wonderful toast, saying, "Paul has been a good friend for a lot of years, and he represents everything that we respect. . . .

He was always a better friend in the down days than in the up days, and that's really the character of a person."

When the governor finished his toast, Paul, a trained opera singer, belted out a song in Italian dedicated to the governor. Then he cut into a *Goodfellas*-themed cake made by the Cake Boss himself, Buddy Valastro. In true mobster style, the cake was decorated with a full-sized gun! That was a party we will never forget.

We sometimes create an at-home Italian Street Festival, to the delight of our friends. We string lights on our terrace to enhance the mood. This menu makes for a colorful buffet—and a great party theme.

Menu

Dee Dee's Special Cocktail:
THE MIDTOWN FOX

STUFFED CLAMS Oreganata
Sausage HERO
Fresh MARGHERITA PIZZA
CALZONES Three Ways
Chocolate Chip TORTA

ALTERNATIVES
PASTA e FAGIOLI
LENTIL Soup

Dee Dee's Special Cocktail

THE MIDTOWN FOX

Serves 1

Our favorite city deserves a fabulous cocktail. I've called this drink the Midtown Fox, because Paul and I met at Fox News in midtown Manhattan. New York City will always be special to us, because it's where we started our wonderful life together. The first Broadway show we saw together was On the Town, *and you know what town it is! Paul loves Frank Sinatra's* "New York, New York," *and my favorite city song is* "Empire State of Mind," *a duet with Alicia Keys and Jay-Z.*

I thought it was appropriate to use gin in my New York cocktail, because the British loyalist stronghold during the American Revolution was New York City. We kicked out the British but kept their alcohol. Thanks, King George!

1 thin cucumber slice (cut lengthwise)
3 ounces gin
½ ounce fresh lemon juice
½ ounce simple syrup
6 dashes El Guapo Cucumber-Lavender Bitters
Club soda

Wrap a cucumber slice around the inside of a highball glass. Fill the glass halfway with ice, making sure that the cucumber slice remains pressed against the interior of the glass. Fill a cocktail shaker halfway with ice. Add the gin, lemon juice, simple syrup, and bitters. Shake vigorously for 5 seconds. Strain the mixture into the highball glass and top off with club soda.

STUFFED CLAMS Oreganata

Serves 6 to 8

Clams oreganata are traditionally served as an appetizer for the Feast of the Seven Fishes, celebrated on Christmas Eve, when Roman Catholics used to abstain from meat. The number seven stands for the seven sacraments of the Roman Catholic Church—or the seven hills of Rome, depending on your point of view.

We offer two serving options: You can serve these baked clams with a spicy red sauce on the side or just sprinkle them with paprika and serve with lemon wedges.

You might want to save all the clamshells so that you can use them again. Clean them and boil them well before storing them. In the future, you can make the same recipe using canned chopped clams.

24 littleneck clams
1½ tablespoons olive oil
2 garlic cloves, minced
1½ cups soft bread crumbs
¼ cup grated Pecorino Romano cheese
½ teaspoon dried oregano
Paprika (optional)
Lemon wedges, for serving (optional)
¼ teaspoon red pepper flakes (optional)
¾ cup Marinara Sauce (page 14; optional)

Preheat the oven to 475°F.

Wash the clams under cold, running water. Discard any open clamshells that do not close when tapped.

Transfer the clams to a large saucepan. Cover and cook the clams over high heat, shaking often, until all the clams open, 3 to 5 minutes. Use a slotted spoon to transfer the clams to a bowl, discarding any that have stayed closed.

Strain the juices in the saucepan through a fine-mesh sieve or several thicknesses of dampened cheesecloth and reserve.

Remove the clams from the shells and chop them. You will use only 12 of the shells; you can boil the leftover shells for use at a later date.

In a medium skillet, heat the olive oil over medium heat. Add the garlic and sauté until fragrant, about a minute.

Remove the skillet from the heat. Add the bread crumbs, cheese, oregano, chopped clams, and 3 tablespoons of the reserved clam juices. Stir to combine well.

Fill the clamshells with the clam mixture and place them on a rimmed baking sheet. If desired, sprinkle some paprika on top of the clams. Bake until the clams are lightly browned and crisp, 8 to 10 minutes. Arrange the clams on a platter surrounded by lemon wedges and serve.

Alternatively, skip the paprika and lemon wedges. While the clams are baking, stir the red pepper flakes and any remaining clam juices into the marinara sauce. Heat the sauce over medium heat until hot, 2 to 3 minutes. To serve, arrange the clams on a platter and pass a bowl of the spicy marinara sauce on the side.

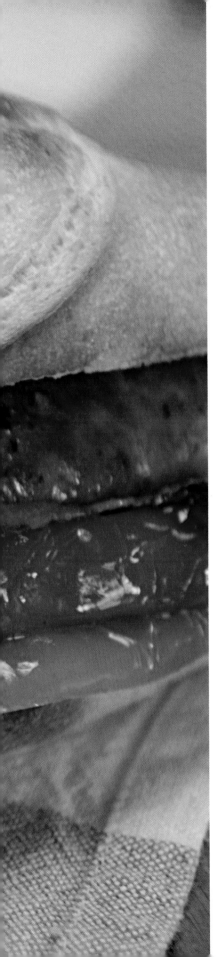

Sausage HERO

Serves 4

A sausage and pepper hero is the best of *Italian street food. I have complemented long, pale green frying peppers with multicolored bell peppers. I think the bell peppers sweeten and intensify the flavor.*

¼ cup olive oil

8 (4-ounce) sweet or hot Italian sausages

4 bell peppers of various colors, seeded and cut into strips (For the green pepper, I like to use an Italian frying pepper.)

1 medium onion, sliced

1 cup Marinara Sauce (page 14)

4 hero rolls, cut in half

In a large skillet, warm the olive oil over medium heat. Add the sausages and fry until browned evenly on all sides. Add the peppers and onion and sauté until soft, 5 to 8 minutes. Add the marinara sauce, reduce the heat to low, and cook for 20 minutes.

Spread some of the pepper mixture on both sides of each roll. Add two sausages, sliced in half, to each and serve.

Fresh MARGHERITA PIZZA

1 (16-inch) pizza

You know you are in New York when you can buy a slice of pie just about anywhere. According to Statistic Brain, Americans consume 3 billion pizzas annually. On any day, one in eight Americans eats pizza, and 93 percent of Americans eat at least one slice of pizza a month. The average number of slices of pizza eaten by a single person in a year is forty-six. All this is to say that we sure love our pizza in the United States! Your guests will especially enjoy this fresh pizza, made with the best ingredients.

1 (14½-ounce) can whole peeled San Marzano tomatoes, drained
2 garlic cloves, minced
1 recipe Paul's Pizza Dough (page 36)
All-purpose flour, for dusting

Cornmeal, for dusting
8 ounces fresh mozzarella, thinly sliced
Fresh basil leaves
Extra-virgin olive oil, for drizzling

If you have a pizza stone, place it in the oven. Preheat the oven to 500°F.

In a small bowl, crush the tomatoes by hand. Stir in the garlic.

If you want to channel your inner Italian, give the dough a toss or two in the air. Dust a work surface well with flour. Hand-press or roll out the pizza dough to the desired shape and thickness.

If using a pizza stone, carefully remove it from the oven. Alternatively, many people who use a pizza stone keep it in the oven at all times, and they use a large wooden pizza spatula (called a "peel") to transfer the pie to the stone. This is a good idea if you plan on making lots of pizzas; you can use a large rimless baking sheet for the same purpose. If you do take your pizza stone in and out of the oven, be very careful since it is heavy and hot. Sprinkle the pizza stone, peel, or baking sheet with cornmeal in order to prevent the dough from sticking.

Place the crust on the pizza stone or baking sheet. Top the crust with the crushed tomatoes, leaving a ½-inch border all around, and lay the slices of mozzarella on the sauce.

Put the pizza stone back in the oven and bake until the pizza crust is golden brown and the cheese is bubbling, about 15–20 minutes.

Remove the pizza from the oven, top with basil leaves, and drizzle with extra-virgin olive oil.

CALZONES Three Ways

Serves 4

*T*his folded pizza, the prototype for a Hot Pocket, originated in Naples. You can be as creative about the filling as you want. I often use leftover vegetables with a little cheese and some sauce in my calzones. It's a perfect lunch!

1 recipe Paul's Pizza Dough (page 36)
Cornmeal, for dusting
Choice of filling (see below)

Preheat the oven to 425°F. Dust a baking sheet with cornmeal to prevent the dough from sticking.

Divide the pizza dough into four pieces and roll each into an 8-inch circles.

Cover half of each dough circle with the filling, leaving a ½-inch border around the edge. Fold the dough over the filling to form a turnover. Press the edges with the tines of a fork to seal.

Transfer the calzones to the baking sheet and bake until the calzones are puffed and golden, about 20 minutes.

FILLINGS

CLASSICO

1 cup ricotta cheese
8 ounces mozzarella cheese,
    cut into cubes
6 cherry tomatoes, sliced
1 teaspoon chopped fresh basil

In a bowl, mix the ricotta, mozzarella, tomatoes, and basil. Proceed with the main recipe.

SPINACH-RICOTTA

10 ounces baby spinach

2 tablespoons olive oil, plus more
   for brushing

1 onion, minced

2 garlic cloves, minced

½ cup grated Parmesan cheese

4 ounces fresh mozzarella cheese, diced

1 cup ricotta cheese

Sea salt

Freshly ground black pepper

Rinse the spinach but do not dry it.

In a large skillet, heat the olive oil over medium heat. Add the onion and cook, stirring occasionally, until translucent, about 4 minutes. Stir in the garlic and cook until fragrant, about 1 minute. Add the spinach, cover, and cook until tender, about 3 minutes.

Drain the spinach mixture in a sieve, pressing gently to remove excess liquid. Transfer to a bowl, add the Parmesan, mozzarella, and ricotta cheeses, and mix well. Season with salt and pepper to taste.

Proceed with the main recipe.

SAUSAGE and CHEESE

4 (4-ounce) sweet or hot Italian sausage

1 cup Marinara Sauce (page 14)

½ teaspoon red pepper flakes

½ teaspoon crushed fennel seeds

1½ cups shredded mozzarella (about 6 ounces)

¼ cup grated Parmesan cheese

Remove the sausage meat from the casings. Crumble the meat into a saucepan and sauté over medium heat until no longer pink, about 10 minutes. Stir in the marinara sauce, red pepper flakes, and fennel seeds. Cook for 5 minutes. Let cool, then skim the fat from the top.

When filling the calzones, cover half of each dough circle with the mozzarella cheese, leaving a ½-inch border around the edge. Top with the sausage mixture and sprinkle with the Parmesan cheese. Proceed with the main recipe.

Chocolate Chip TORTA

Serves 8 to 12

A torta is a rustic cake. This chocolate chip ricotta torta combines a crumble crust and topping with a creamy cheesecake that resembles cannoli filling. Enjoy this traditional Italian cake on its own or topped with gelato or nuts.

FOR THE CRUST:

8 ounces (2 sticks) cold unsalted butter, cut into pieces, plus more at room temperature for greasing the pan

2½ cups all-purpose flour, plus more for dusting the pan

1 cup sugar

1½ teaspoons baking powder

2 large eggs

1 tablespoon whole milk

1 tablespoon Frangelico

FOR THE FILLING:

8 ounces ricotta cheese

8 ounces mascarpone cheese

2 large eggs

1 cup sugar

1 cup semisweet chocolate chips

Preheat the oven to 350°F.

Grease a 9-inch springform pan with butter and dust with flour, then tap out the excess flour. Set aside.

To make the crust for the bottom and the crumble for the top:

In a large mixing bowl, whisk together the flour, sugar, and baking powder.

In a small bowl, beat together the eggs, milk, and Frangelico. Use a fork to combine this mixture with the flour mixture.

With a fork or your fingers, work pieces of cold butter gently into the mixture. The finished product will resemble a crumble when done. Gently pat half the crumble mixture into the bottom of the prepared pan and set aside.

To make the filling: In a large mixing bowl, whisk together the ricotta, mascarpone, eggs, and sugar. Fold in the chocolate chips until they are evenly distributed.

Spread the filling over the crust in the pan. Scatter the remaining crumble over the filling, covering it completely. Bake until a toothpick inserted in the center comes out clean, 50 to 60 minutes. Cool to room temperature before removing from the springform pan.

PASTA e FAGIOLI

Serves 8

If you know any Italian-Americans, you have probably heard this dish referred to as "pasta fazool." In my family, it was served on Friday nights, followed by fried fish, because Fridays were meatless then. I still associate this wonderful pasta dish with the feeling that the work week was over.

3 tablespoons olive oil

3 garlic cloves, chopped

⅓ (10-ounce) can crushed Italian tomatoes in puree

3 (16-ounce) cans cannellini beans

1 pound small pasta shells or ditalini

Sea salt

Freshly ground black pepper

Put a large pot of salted water on the stove to boil for the pasta.

In another large pot, heat the oil over medium heat. Add the garlic and cook for 3-4 minutes until golden brown. Do not burn the garlic.

Add the tomatoes and beans. When it starts to simmer turn heat to low until beans are soft, approximately 45 minutes. Stir occasionally.

Cook pasta al dente, per instructions on the box.

When bean mixture is ready, add pasta. Stir until it reaches the consistency of chili, or as my Aunt Mary used to call it, "gloomy." Note: this dish is ruined by adding cheese. Add salt and pepper to taste.

Alternative

LENTIL Soup

Serves 4

L entils are so nutrient dense that this soup is a meal in itself. When I was a child, it was a meatless Friday mainstay, but now I like to add some chopped bacon as a topping for extra flavor. For a satisfying meal, serve a bowl of this soup with crusty bread and a salad.

½ cup dried lentils

2 medium carrots, peeled and chopped

1 celery stalk, chopped

1 garlic clove, peeled but left whole

3 tablespoons chopped seeded tomato

¼ teaspoon dried oregano

1 (3-by-1-inch) slice salt pork or pancetta

3 cups water

1 small potato, peeled and diced

1 teaspoon chopped fresh flat-leaf parsley, for serving

Sea salt

Freshly ground black pepper

Grated Parmesan cheese, for serving

8 ounces sliced bacon or pancetta, cooked and crumbled, for topping (optional)

In a large pot, combine the lentils, carrots, celery, garlic clove, tomato, oregano, salt pork, and water. Cook over low heat, stirring occasionally, for 1½ hours.

Add the potato and cook until tender, about 20 minutes. Add salt and pepper to taste. Ladle into soup bowls and sprinkle each serving with parsley, Parmesan, and crumbled bacon (if desired).

LA-LA LAND

Hooray for Hollywood!

DEE DEE: If you told me three years ago that I would marry an actor and live in Los Angeles for part of the year, I would have said you were crazy. But I discovered that I loved Paul so much, I would follow him anywhere. And Los Angeles is important for Paul's work. Most of his movie and TV deals are made there.

PAUL: As much as we love New York, when we're trying to get a cab on a cold, blustery day and all we have is a copy of the slim Saturday *New York Times* for protection, we long for the fine weather in Los Angeles. Living is easy there. Culture can be found in Los Angeles—there's television and movies and a big piece of the glamor pie that everyone is trying to get. The city is full of absolutely brilliant people who are there for the same reasons I am. I'm surrounded by my friends and colleagues.

DEE DEE: When I'm in Los Angeles, I have to admit that I miss walking everywhere. I am trying to get Paul to let me buy a bike, but he says that people really don't walk or ride bikes in Los Angeles—they drive everywhere. Sunning by the pool is for Angelenos, but I am so fair that I need big hats and lots of sunscreen to protect myself from skin cancer, which I've already had. I keep reminding myself that Los Angeles has beautiful weather, day after day after day . . . and of course Paul.

PAUL: I do know the city well. When I was eight, we left the East Coast and moved to Los

> "People from Los Angeles put a premium on fresh food. It's so easy to find, there is an abundance we can find year round at farmers' markets."
>
> —PAUL

Angeles and then back to New York City two years later. Los Angeles holds bittersweet memories for me because my parents separated a year later. Yet, it's easy for me to find inspiration in that magnificent weather, and I work well there, particularly on my sculpture.

DEE DEE: When we're not cooking or throwing parties at home, we go out to the Hollywood favorites including Spago, the Ivy, and Shutters on the Beach. We often have parties on our terrace. The backdrop of Los Angeles—and our special Los Angeles cocktail—put us in the mood to enjoy life and not worry about tomorrow.

PAUL: People from Los Angeles put a premium on fresh food. It's so easy to find, there is an abundance we can find year round at farmers' markets. It reminds me of Italy. Farm to table is easy in Los Angeles.

Dee Dee's Special Cocktail
THE HOLLYWOOD STAR
Serves 1

For our Los Angeles get-togethers, we tend to go bright and sunny—with a touch of glamor. That's why I named our Los Angeles drink the Hollywood Star. It looks like a sunny day or the flash of paparazzi cameras. We want to make everyone feel like a star when drinking a cocktail that deserves its own star on Hollywood Boulevard. I recommend serving this drink with a straw to make it even more festive.

1 thin grapefruit slice
2 ounces blanco tequila
¼ ounce Campari
¼ ounce fresh orange juice
2 ounces grapefruit soda
1 maraschino cherry (with stem)

Place the grapefruit slice along the inside wall of a martini glass. Fill the glass with ice, taking care to keep the grapefruit slice pressed against the glass. Fill a cocktail shaker halfway with ice. Add the tequila, Campari, and orange juice. Cover and shake for 5 seconds. Strain into the martini glass. Add the grapefruit soda and garnish with the cherry.

Menu

Dee Dee's Special Cocktail:
THE HOLLYWOOD STAR

Asparagus DIP

FIGS in a Blanket

California VEGGIE PIZZA

SWORDFISH with Olives

PASTA Primavera

Watercress, Pear, and Walnut SALAD
with Balsamic Glaze

Orange POLENTA CUPCAKES
with Cream Cheese Frosting

ALTERNATIVE

EGGS in Purgatory

Stuffed PEPPERS

Asparagus DIP

Serves 4 to 6

T*his simple dip is a beautiful, appealing green that brightens any table. We serve it with crudité, crusty French bread, thin breadsticks, or gluten-free crackers for the Hollywood crowd.*

1 pound asparagus, ends trimmed
1 (8-ounce) package cream cheese, at room temperature
¼ cup grated Parmesan cheese
1 teaspoon chopped fresh dill or chives (optional)
Sea salt
Freshly ground black pepper

Bring a large pot of salted water to a boil over high heat. Add the asparagus and blanch for 3 minutes, then drain and transfer immediately to a cold-water bath.

When cool, cut the asparagus into 1½-inch pieces and set the tips aside.

In a blender or food processor, combine the asparagus pieces (not the tips), cream cheese, Parmesan cheese, and dill or chives, if using. Pulse to reach the desired consistency—the dip can be chunky or smooth. Add salt and pepper to taste.

Transfer the dip to a serving bowl and fold in the asparagus tips by hand.

FIGS in a Blanket

Serves 6

The combination of sweet fresh figs and salty prosciutto is hard to resist. Though this appetizer takes very little preparation time, our guests are always impressed.

12 thin slices prosciutto (about 4 ounces), cut lengthwise into 1-inch strips
12 large ripe figs, halved lengthwise
Olive oil

Preheat the oven to 425°F. Line a rimmed baking sheet with parchment paper.

Wrap a strip of prosciutto around the widest part of each fig half, with the ends overlapping.

Arrange the figs, cut-side up, on the lined baking sheet. Brush the figs with olive oil.

Roast until the figs are warm and the prosciutto is crisp, about 10 minutes.

California VEGGIE PIZZA
Serves 4 to 6

A *pizza smothered in vegetables is perfect for the California crowd and health-conscious people everywhere. I like to put together an unusual medley of vegetables that are not commonly seen on pizza, and you can choose to add cheese or not.*

Cornmeal, for dusting
1 recipe Paul's Pizza Dough (page 36)
1 tablespoon unsalted butter
12 asparagus spears, cut into 1½-inch pieces, tips reserved
½ cup Marinara Sauce (page 14)
1½ cups shredded mozzarella cheese
1 red onion, thinly sliced
½ cup pitted green olives
½ cup pitted black olives
4 ounces shiitake mushroom, sliced
1 small can whole baby corn, drained
1 yellow bell pepper, seeded and thinly sliced
1 bunch scallions, sliced

Preheat the oven to 475°F. Dust a pizza stone or baking sheet with cornmeal.

Dust a work surface well with cornmeal and roll out the pizza dough. Transfer the dough to the pizza stone or baking sheet.

In small skillet, melt the butter over medium heat and lightly sauté the asparagus until tender, 4 to 5 minutes.

Spread the marinara sauce on the pizza crust, leaving a ½-inch border. Scatter the mozzarella on the sauce.

Arrange the asparagus, onion, olives, mushrooms, corn, yellow pepper, and scallions on top.

Bake until the cheese is melted and bubbling and the crust turns golden, 12 to 15 minutes.

SWORDFISH with Olives

Serves 4

We enjoy many types of fish and shellfish, but swordfish is one of our favorites. Its mildly sweet flavor and meaty texture make it very versatile. Though this recipe is very simple to make, the blend of flavors creates a standout centerpiece for your meal.

½ cup olive oil
⅓ cup capers, drained
24 pitted Kalamata olives
½ medium onion, sliced
4 (6-ounce) swordfish steaks (about 1 inch thick)
4 large or 8 small basil leaves, cut into ribbons
Lemon wedges, for serving

In a large skillet, warm the olive oil over medium heat. Add the capers, olives, onion, basil and sauté for 5 minutes.

Place the swordfish steaks on top of the mixture. Raise the heat to medium and cook for 5 minutes on each side. (Alternatively, you can grill the swordfish on an outdoor grill for 5 minutes on each side.)

Transfer the swordfish steaks to a serving dish. Scrape the pan and cover swordfish with olive mixture. Serve with lemon wedges.

PASTA Primavera

Serves 4 to 6

The beauty of this dish is that you can use any vegetables you wish. You can sauté, steam, or roast them—just make sure your ingredients are fresh and the pasta will be delicious! Our recipe calls for roasting the veggies and then tossing them with the pasta and oil. Simple, classic, and bursting with flavor.

1 pound asparagus, trimmed and cut in half

3 carrots, peeled and cut into long strips with a vegetable peeler

2 medium zucchini, sliced

2 medium yellow summer squash, sliced

½ cup olive oil, divided

⅛ teaspoon dried oregano

1 tablespoon dried parsley

Sea salt

Freshly ground black pepper

1 pound penne

1 bunch scallions (white and light green parts only), chopped

½ cup grated Parmesan cheese

Preheat the oven to 450°F. Line two large rimmed baking sheets with aluminum foil.

Put a large pot of salted water on the stove to boil for the pasta.

Combine the asparagus, carrots, zucchini, and yellow squash in a zip-top plastic bag. Add ¼ cup of the oil, the dried herbs, and salt and pepper to taste. Toss well to coat.

Spread out the vegetables in a single layer on the lined baking sheets. Bake, turning the vegetables once, until they begin to brown, 15 to 20 minutes.

Meanwhile, cook the pasta according to the package directions until al dente. Drain, reserving 1 cup of the cooking liquid.

In a large bowl, toss the pasta with the roasted vegetables and scallions. Add the remaining ¼ cup olive oil and the reserved cooking liquid to moisten. Season with salt and pepper to taste. Sprinkle with the Parmesan and serve.

Watercress, Pear, and Walnut SALAD with Balsamic Glaze
Serves 6 to 8

T*his refreshing salad is one of our favorites. The crunch factor is high, the blend of flavors is delicious, and the salad looks great on the plate.*

1 cup balsamic vinegar

3 pears, cored, and cut into chunks or thinly sliced

4 cups watercress leaves

3 bunches arugula

Sea salt

Freshly ground black pepper

½ cup crumbled gorgonzola cheese, crumbled goat cheese, or cubed fontina cheese

½ cup chopped walnuts

Pour the balsamic vinegar into a saucepan and cook over medium-low heat until reduced to ½ cup, about 15 minutes.

Combine the pears, watercress, and arugula in a large serving bowl.

Drizzle with the balsamic glaze and toss to coat. Season with salt and pepper to taste.

Scatter the crumbled cheese and walnuts on top.

Orange POLENTA CUPCAKES with Cream Cheese Frosting

Makes 12 cupcakes

These delicious cupcakes are an orangey delight. If you like, you can top the frosting with candied orange peel.

FOR THE CUPCAKES:

2 cups cake flour or all-purpose flour

¾ cup fine polenta

1½ teaspoons baking powder

16 tablespoons (2 sticks) unsalted butter

1 cup sugar

3 large eggs

Grated zest of 3 large oranges

FOR THE FROSTING:

1 pound cream cheese

5 tablespoons unsalted butter, at room temperature

1 cup confectioners' sugar

Juice of 1 lemon

To make the cupcakes, preheat the oven to 350°F. Line a 12-cup muffin tin with paper or silicone cupcake liners.

In a bowl, whisk together the flour, polenta, and baking powder.

In the bowl of an electric mixer, beat the butter and sugar until fluffy. With the mixer going, add one-third of the dry ingredients. Add 1 egg. Repeat by alternating the dry ingredients and the remaining 2 eggs. Add the orange zest and beat until smooth.

Using an ice cream scoop or a large spoon, place a scoop of the mixture in each cupcake liner. Bake until a toothpick stuck in the center comes out dry, about 25 minutes.

Allow the cupcakes to cool before frosting.

To make the frosting, in the bowl of an electric mixer, cream together the cream cheese and butter on low speed. Do not overmix. Mix in the sugar until just combined, adding the lemon juice at the end. Frost the cupcakes.

EGGS in Purgatory

Serves 6

Alternative

In *this dish, eggs are simmered in a red sauce. The symbolism is right out of Dante's* Divine Comedy. *Some say the eggs represent souls in* Purgatorio *seeking purification so that they can go to* Paradiso. *Neapolitans have long been preoccupied with* Purgatorio, *where souls are trapped between heaven and hell. Scenes from purgatory are painted in seventeenth-century churches throughout Naples.*

2 tablespoons olive oil

3 garlic cloves, minced

1 (14-ounce) can pureed San Marzano tomatoes

1 (14-ounce) can diced San Marzano tomatoes

6 large eggs

¼ cup chopped fresh flat-leaf parsley

Freshly ground black pepper

Toasted Italian bread, for dipping

Heat the olive oil in a large skillet over medium-high heat. Add the garlic and sauté about 5 minutes.

Stir in the diced tomatoes with their juices and bring to a boil. The mixture must be hot enough to poach the eggs.

Using the back of a spoon, make six little wells in the tomato mixture, one for each egg.

Carefully crack an egg into each well. Reduce the heat to medium-low. Cover the skillet and allow the eggs to poach for about 5 minutes. The whites should be cooked through, while the yolks should still be runny. Sprinkle with parsley and a few grinds of black pepper and serve with toasted Italian bread.

Stuffed PEPPERS

Serves 8

Alternative

*A*platter of these colorful stuffed peppers always gets attention. They can be served as a first course or as a main course. This comfort food is a good way to use up leftover meat or vegetables. The recipe is forgiving, so feel free to make substitutions or additions to your own taste.

2 tablespoons olive oil

8 large bell peppers (preferably a mix of green, red, yellow, and orange)

1 pound lean ground beef

1 pound sweet Italian sausage, casings removed

1 onion, diced

3 large eggs, lightly beaten

2 teaspoons sea salt

1 teaspoon freshly ground black pepper

1 cup chopped fresh flat-leaf parsley leaves (reserve some for garnish)

1 cup chopped fresh basil leaves

2 cups cooked white rice

2 cups Marinara Sauce (page 14)

½ to 1 cup ricotta

Preheat the oven to 400°F.

Use the olive oil to coat the bottom of a baking pan large enough to fit the peppers standing upright.

Cut the tops off of the peppers and remove the seeds and ribs.

In a large mixing bowl, mix the ground beef, Italian sausage, onion, eggs, salt, and pepper with your hands. Add the parsley, basil, and rice and mix until thoroughly combined.

Divide the stuffing equally among the peppers, leaving room for a layer of ricotta cheese on top. Place the peppers in the pan and cover with marinara sauce. Fill the top of each pepper with ricotta.

Bake until the peppers are tender and browned, 45 to 60 minutes.

SING FOR OUR SUPPER

5

"He plays the piano and sings every day,
to my immense pleasure."

—DEE DEE

From La Scala to the Catskills

PAUL: When my mother was a teenager, she played the piano at a silent movie house. She was such a brilliant musician that she was offered a scholarship to Juilliard. Her parents were old-school wealthy Italians and would not let her accept the offer. It was heartless. By the time I was born, she was a music teacher. Her students practiced and took lessons in our house. The first sound I distinctly remember is piano music.

I had a cousin, much older than I, who had a beautiful tenor voice and sung at La Scala, the great opera house in Milan. At a very young age, I knew I wanted to be like him, to go on stage as he did. I developed a singing voice at the age of seven and haven't stopped singing since. I didn't take up the piano until much later.

I loved Mario Lanza, Enrico Caruso, and Frank Sinatra. At thirteen, I won an Italian speaking contest at Columbia University. My prize was literature by Dante and a recording of Puccini's *La Bohème.* I listened to those beautiful Puccini arias every day after school. I also loved the albums of the great Broadway musicals of the time—Mary Martin and Ezio Pinza in *South Pacific,* Yul Brynner and Deborah Kerr in the *The King and I,* Rex Harrison in *My Fair Lady,* Carol Lawrence and Chita Rivera in *West Side Story.* It was the golden age of musical theater.

When I was sixteen, I went to work as a singer in a resort hotel named Perella's Maple Leaf in the Italian section of the Catskills known as the "minestrone belt." I was paid twenty-five dollars a week plus room and board. The following year I worked as a social director "tummler" at a Jewish resort in the Borscht Belt called the Alamac. I performed all day into the night usually eighteen hours. Not even the Army was as grueling, but I was in heaven. It was a job I was born for.

DEE DEE: During Oscar week one year, we ran into Alec Baldwin outside Montage Beverly Hills. Paul broke into song, as he often does. Several months later Alec invited Paul to introduce the New York philharmonic and be special guest the night they played *The Godfather* score. New Yorkers love their big Paulie and Alec Baldwin was brilliant to call on Paul.

Paul's music is as important to him as his acting. He plays the piano and sings every day, to my immense pleasure. He had his own special on PBS and sang at a gala at the Metropolitan Opera and on the recordings of three Broadway shows. He had the leading role in *Most Happy Fella,* which was staged by the New York City Opera.

When we plan a menu, we try to emulate the harmony and flow of great music. If it all works together—color, texture, flavor, aroma—the enjoyment factor increases exponentially and makes a lasting impression.

We dedicated the special cocktail for this feast, Marietta's Song, to Paul's beautiful and accomplished mother.

Dee Dee's Special Cocktail
MARIETTA'S SONG
Serves 1

We named the drink for our music chapter after Paul's mother, Marietta.

I wanted to keep this drink simple and elegant, just like Paul's mom. Marietta's Song is a beautiful, jewel-toned drink in an old-fashioned Champagne glass. Champagne is the only possible drink for a woman of such grace, energy, and beauty.

1¼ ounces pomegranate juice

¾ ounce simple syrup

½ ounce rose water

5 ounces champagne

Fill a cocktail shaker one-quarter of the way with ice. Add the pomegranate juice, simple syrup, and rose water. Cover and shake for 5 seconds. Strain into a Champagne glass. Top with the Champagne.

Menu

Dee Dee's Special Cocktail:
MARIETTA'S SONG

BRUSCHETTA with Roasted Red Peppers and Mozzarella

BRUSCHETTA with Caramelized Onions, Mushrooms,
and Roasted Garlic

LINGUINE con Vongole

Shrimp SCAMPI

Roasted BROCCOLI RABE with Garlic and Lemon Zest

Nancy's Chocolate Coffee MOUSSE

ALTERNATIVE

Our Favorite VEAL STEW

BRUSCHETTA Two Ways

*B*ruschetta, pronounced "broo-sketta," refers to toasted bread. You are probably familiar with the tomato, basil, olive oil, and balsamic vinegar version served on toast in most Italian restaurants in the States as an appetizer. In Italy, bruschetta is topped with many delectable combinations of ingredients. Here are two of our favorites.

BRUSCHETTA with Roasted Red Peppers and Mozzarella

*R*oasting peppers intensifies their sweet flavor, which works well with the mild mozzarella. We never seem to make enough of this bruschetta—a platter goes very quickly when we have people over.

1 baguette, thinly sliced

Extra-virgin olive oil

1 garlic clove, cut in half

4 red bell peppers, roasted (see page 128), peeled, seeded, and thinly sliced,
   or 1 (16-ounce) jar roasted red peppers, drained and thinly sliced

1 onion, chopped (optional)

1 cup chopped fresh basil

1 tablespoon balsamic vinegar

8 ounces fresh mozzarella, thinly sliced

Preheat the broiler.

Brush the bread on one side with olive oil. Rub each side of the bread with the cut side of the garlic. Place the bread on a baking sheet and broil until golden. Remove the pan from the broiler and let the bread cool.

In a medium bowl, toss together the roasted peppers, onion (if using), basil, and vinegar. Spoon some of the mixture on each piece of bread.

Place a few strips of mozzarella diagonally on top of the roasted pepper mixture. Drizzle with extra-virgin olive oil.

Broil the bruschetta until the cheese melts and browns.

BRUSCHETTA with Caramelized Onions, Mushrooms, and Roasted Garlic
Serves 8

This variation of bruschetta has a mouth-watering aroma. Our place smells wonderful when we make this recipe—a promise of the good food to come for our guests.

1 baguette, thinly sliced

2 tablespoons olive oil, divided, plus more for brushing the bread

½ sweet yellow onion, thinly sliced

8 ounces button or cremini mushrooms, sliced

½ head roasted garlic (see page 128)

Sea salt

Freshly ground black pepper

Preheat the broiler.

Brush the bread on one side with some of the olive oil. Place the bread on a baking sheet and broil until golden. Remove the pan from the broiler and let the bread cool.

In a large skillet, heat 1 tablespoon of the olive oil over medium heat. Add the onion and sauté until caramelized, 15 to 20 minutes. Use a slotted spoon to transfer the onion to a plate.

Add the remaining 1 tablespoon olive oil to the skillet and reheat. Add the mushrooms and sauté until golden brown, 5 to 7 minutes. Return the onions to the pan and add the roasted garlic. Cook until heated through. Season with salt and pepper to taste.

Spoon some of the mixture onto each of the bread slices and serve.

How to Roast Peppers

*I*t's worth the time to roast bell peppers yourself. The flavor is deeper and the texture more velvety than roasted peppers from a jar.

Preheat the oven to 450°F.

Put a wire rack on a baking sheet and place the whole bell peppers on the rack. Roast the peppers, turning them now and then with tongs, until they blacken in spots, 30 to 40 minutes.

Transfer the roasted peppers to a large bowl and cover with plastic wrap. Let the peppers steam for 10 minutes. Uncover and let the peppers cool.

Remove the stems, skins, and seeds with a paring knife and cut the peppers into thin slices.

How to Roast Garlic

*T*his is a recipe you should have under your belt. Roasted garlic has a million uses and adds great flavor to everything. We mix it with mustard or mayonnaise and use it as a spread. Roasted garlic also peps up mashed potatoes, roasted veggies, soups, salads, pasta, and even mac and cheese.

1 head garlic, outer paper leaves removed
1 to 2 teaspoons olive oil

Preheat the oven to 400°F.

Cut straight across the top of the garlic head about ½ inch down. Cut off the tops of the cloves but leave the bulb intact.

Put the garlic head in a ramekin, drizzle with olive oil, and cover with aluminum foil, or simply put the garlic head on a piece of foil, drizzle with the oil, and seal the foil well.

Roast the garlic until tender and lightly browned, 30 to 40 minutes. Remove from the oven and allow to cool.

Squeeze the garlic out of its skin into a small dish. Slice or mash with a fork and use as desired.

LINGUINE con Vongole

Serves 6 to 8

T*his classic pasta dish from Naples is often served at Christmas as a course for the Feast of the Seven Fishes. Easy as can be, the recipe calls for simply steaming the clams in wine with garlic and red pepper flakes. The juices from the clams flavor the broth-like sauce. As is always the case with seafood, the fresher the clams, the more delicious this dish will be. Manila or littleneck clams are good choices for this dish, but any smaller fresh clam will work.*

1 pound linguine
¼ cup olive oil
5 garlic cloves, slivered
½ teaspoon red pepper flakes
2½ pounds fresh clams, scrubbed
Sea salt
1 cup chopped fresh flat-leaf parsley
Freshly ground black pepper

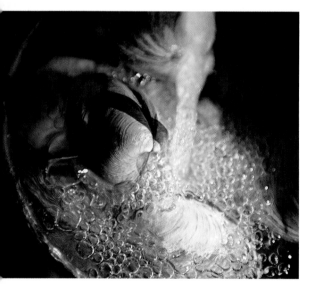

Put a large pot of salted water on the stove to boil. Add the linguine and cook until al dente, 10 to 12 minutes. Drain.

While the pasta is cooking, heat the olive oil in a large skillet over medium-high heat. Add the garlic and red pepper flakes and sauté for 2 minutes. Add the clams and cover the pan. Cook until the clams open and release their juices, 4 to 6 minutes. Discard any clams that do not open.

Add the drained linguine to the skillet and toss to coat the pasta with the clam juices.

Season with salt to taste. Toss with the parsley and serve with a few grinds of black pepper.

Shrimp SCAMPI
Serves 6

S hrimp scampi is another traditional course for the Christmas Eve Feast of the Seven Fishes. Originally, scampi was the name of a lobster-like crustacean found in Europe that was cooked in its own juices. When Italian immigrants came to the States, they adapted the recipe to use the local shrimp. Today, "scampi" has become synonymous with shrimp. Italian cooks in the early twentieth century used whatever ingredients were available, so there is a wide range of ways to make this dish. I like to stick with the classic version using wine, lemon, red pepper flakes, and parsley.

½ cup olive oil
4 garlic cloves, minced
½ cup dry white wine
⅛ teaspoon red pepper flakes
Sea salt
Freshly ground black pepper
1¾ pounds large or extra-large shrimp, peeled and deveined
⅓ cup chopped fresh flat-leaf parsley
Juice of ½ lemon
Cooked pasta or crusty bread, for serving

Heat the olive oil in a large skillet over medium heat. Add the garlic and sauté for 1 minute. Add the wine and red pepper flakes, season with salt and pepper to taste, and bring to a simmer. Simmer until the wine is reduced by half, about 2 minutes.

Add the shrimp and sauté until they turn pink, 2 to 4 minutes. Stir in the parsley and lemon juice.

Serve the shrimp over pasta or with crusty bread.

Roasted BROCCOLI RABE with Garlic

Serves 4 to 6

Italians love greens, and broccoli rabe is one of the most nutrient dense foods you can eat. I have learned that it is important not to chop the leaves, which releases bitter enzymes. Roasting or broiling broccoli rabe cuts the bitterness and accentuates its nutty, zesty flavor.

1 pound broccoli rabe, tough stems removed
2 tablespoons olive oil
2 garlic cloves, minced
Sea salt
½ teaspoon red pepper flakes

Preheat the oven to 425°F.

Toss the broccoli rabe with the olive oil, garlic, a pinch of sea salt, and red pepper flakes and spread in a roasting pan. Roast for 10 minutes.

Transfer the roasted broccoli rabe to a serving dish.

Nancy's Chocolate Coffee MOUSSE

Serves 6 to 8

*M*ousse is always a special treat after a good meal. This recipe is streamlined, so you can put this rich mousse together in a snap. It does need at least 3 hours to set, so you should keep that in mind when planning a meal. The good news is that you can make it a day ahead and have dessert ready in the refrigerator—except for the whipped cream, which you can make just before serving. Or skip the whipped cream and serve the mousse as is, with biscotti. Dee Dee's mom loves her chocolate and coffee.

½ cup whole milk
2 tablespoons sugar
2 tablespoons coffee liqueur
1 cup chopped dark chocolate (minimum 60% cacao)
3 extra-large egg whites
Heavy whipping cream (optional)

Heat the milk in a saucepan over low heat. Add the sugar and liqueur and stir until the sugar has completely dissolved. Do not let the milk boil. Put the chopped chocolate in a blender. Pour the heated milk sauce over the chocolate and blend for 1 minute on low to medium. Add the egg whites and blend on high until the mixture is light and makes soft peaks, 1 to 2 minutes.

Spoon the mixture into individual serving dishes or wine glasses. Cover and refrigerate for at least 3 hours or overnight.

If desired, whip the cream with sugar to taste until stiff peaks form and spoon on top of the mousse.

Our Favorite VEAL STEW

Serves 4 to 6

2 pounds boneless veal shoulder, trimmed and cut into 2-inch pieces

1 teaspoon sea salt, divided

½ teaspoon freshly ground black pepper, divided

¼ cup all-purpose flour

2 to 3 tablespoons olive oil

1 medium onion, chopped

1 cup chicken stock or canned broth

½ cup dry white wine

1 (14-ounce) whole peeled San Marzano tomatoes, drained and chopped

¼ teaspoon dried oregano

1 (10-ounce) package frozen peas

1 recipe Roasted Potatoes (page 196; optional)

Season the veal with ½ teaspoon of the salt and ¼ teaspoon of the pepper. Dredge the veal in the flour, shaking off the excess.

Heat 2 tablespoons olive oil in a Dutch oven over medium-high heat. Add the veal and cook until lightly browned on all sides, 5 to 7 minutes. Do not crowd the veal; you may have to do this is two batches. Remove the browned veal with a slotted spoon and set aside.

If the pan is dry, add 1 more tablespoon olive oil. Add the onion and cook over medium heat until softened, 2 to 3 minutes.

Return the veal to the Dutch oven. Add the stock, wine, tomatoes, oregano, and remaining ½ teaspoon salt and ¼ teaspoon pepper. Bring to a boil, reduce the heat to medium-low, cover, and simmer until the veal is tender, about 1 hour.

Add the peas and roasted potatoes (if using) and simmer until heated through, about 5 minutes.

A GOODFELLAS FEAST

"At school, I was always the class actor. The desire to
be on stage pervaded every moment of my life."

—PAUL

I am Paul. Paul Oatmeal.

PAUL: My acting career began in a kindergarten play when I was five years old. I remember my lines to this day: "I am Paul. Paul oatmeal. True of heart and true of soul, put me in your breakfast bowl."

DEE DEE: The role was a perfect combination of two of his favorite things: acting and food! Clearly a star was born on that school stage.

PAUL: At school, I was always the class actor. The desire to be on stage pervaded every moment of my life. I worked in a movie theater near home just so that I could see movies without paying admission.

After appearing in just under 200 films, I still believe that the collaborative process known as moviemaking is today's premier art form.

DEE DEE: When Paul and I had just begun to date, he invited me to see a theater production of *King Lear,* which he was directing and starring in. I was with a friend who was not into Shakespeare. We stayed for a few minutes and then left to get Champagne. I made sure I was back in time to stand in the lobby to wait for him. I would never do that now. I am impressed by everything he does so well.

PAUL: I have always loved the stage. There is something about a live performance that is incomparable. I had a once-in-a-lifetime role in Jason Miller's *That Championship Season* at the Public Theater in 1972. That play made my career, especially after numerous rave reviews and one extraordinary review in the Sunday edition of the *New York Times.*

DEE DEE: I was thrilled to be at the 25th anniversary event for *Goodfellas* that closed the Tribeca Film Festival in 2015. Following a screening of Martin Scorsese's classic film, Jon Stewart hosted a panel with Paul, Ray Liotta, Robert De Niro, Lorraine Bracco, and Nicholas Pileggi, who wrote the book and screenplay.

Paul is best known for his iconic role as Paul Cicero, an intimidating capo who could have someone killed just by nodding his head. That evening, Paul told Jon Stewart how close he came to abandoning the movie.

PAUL: Just days before Scorsese was ready to start filming, I was having second thoughts about playing Big Paulie. I, who love opera, poetry, and cooking, was having a hard time putting myself into this lethal guy's shoes. I called my manager and said, "Get me out of this—I can't do it."

My mind changed soon after, as I was fixing my tie in front of the mirror. Looking at my reflection, I saw that guy. Just like that, I saw myself as the criminal Cicero. To be honest, it stunned me out. But that's what acting is all about.

DEE DEE: Since we met, we have appeared in a number of films together. Paul says I'm a natural. I've always had a foot in politics and a foot in entertainment. I'm having a wonderful time. Making a movie is always a great party!

The menu for this chapter consists of a feast fit for "the Boss." The meal is over the top with a selection of classic Italian food that would satisfy even the most demanding Mafia don.

Dee Dee's Special Cocktail
THE GOODFELLA
Serves 1

Paul is recognized almost every day as the boss in Goodfellas and is the ultimate goodfella in life and in the movies. *If you think about it, Paul is the only goodfella in the film. The other guys cheated on their friends and wives and were snitches. Paul was the beloved patriarch, who was loyal to his wife and told Henry Hill he had to go back to his wife. He also helped Henry out with money even after Henry got into the drug business. Big Paulie was good to all, except maybe those wise guys he whacked—but, hey, they had it coming!*

The Goodfella cocktail is strong like Big Paulie: four shots of alcohol in a perfect blend. It is also a nod to Frank Sinatra who Paul says sang "perfectly."

1 ounce Jack Daniel's whiskey
1 ounce Scotch
1 ounce Cognac
½ ounce limoncello
Oversized ice cube
Lemon wedge, for garnish

Fill a cocktail shaker one-quarter full with ice. Add the Jack Daniel's whiskey, Scotch, Cognac, and limoncello. Using a bar spoon, stir in a figure-8 motion for 5 seconds. Strain into a highball glass with one large ice cube. Garnish with the lemon wedge.

Menu

Dee Dee's Special Cocktail:
THE GOODFELLA

Chef Paul's PEPPERS AND OLIVES
ZUPPA di PESCE
LASAGNA alla Mamma
PORCHETTA
Roasted Summer VEGETABLES
ZABAGLIONE with Strawberries and Blueberries
Almond BISCOTTI
Chocolate Chip BISCOTTI

ALTERNATIVE
SPAGHETTI Carbonara

Chef Paul's PEPPERS AND OLIVES

Serves 5

T*his appetizer makes for a terrific light starter if there's a feast to follow. We like to serve it with chunks of crusty bread.*

5 frying peppers
½ cup olive oil
¼ teaspoon red pepper flakes
4 garlic cloves, sliced
⅓ cup pitted Kalamata olives
¼ cup seasoned Italian bread crumbs

Cut off both ends of the peppers and cut them in half lengthwise. Remove the ribs and seeds. Cut the peppers into ¾-inch-thick slices.

In a 12-inch skillet, warm the oil over medium heat. Add the peppers and cook for 45 minutes, turning the peppers every 10 minutes. Add the red pepper flakes, garlic, and olives. Sauté until the garlic is the color of toast. Dust with the bread crumbs.

ZUPPA di PESCE

Serves 4

Thisis a showstopper! *Zuppa di pesce is an irresistible Neapolitan seafood soup/stew that is as gorgeous as it is flavorful. In a narrow country surrounded by the sea, fish is always readily available. They say this dish developed as a convenient way to use all the unsold pieces of the fishermen's daily catch in the time before refrigeration. At the end of the day, anything that was left was thrown into a pot to simmer with some water or white wine and a handful of herbs and spices. When the tomato became a mainstay of Italian cooking, particularly in the South, local versions of fish soup took on various shades of red.*

6 tablespoons olive oil, divided

1 medium onion, coarsely chopped

3 cups chopped fresh or canned tomatoes

½ cup dry white wine (do not use wine you would not drink)

¼ teaspoon dried oregano

1 tablespoon chopped fresh mint

4 tablespoons chopped fresh flat-leaf parsley, divided

Red pepper flakes (optional)

1½ pounds monkfish, cut into 2-inch pieces

12 mussels, scrubbed

8 cherrystone clams, scrubbed

1½ pounds white fish fillets, such as red snapper, bass, or cod, cut into 2-inch pieces

8 ounces jumbo shrimp, peeled and deveined

2 cups fresh bread, cut into ½-inch cubes

2 scallions, cut into 1-inch pieces

Heat 3 tablespoons of the olive oil in a medium saucepan over medium heat. Add the onion and sauté for about 5 minutes.

Add the tomatoes, wine, oregano, mint, 2 tablespoons of the parsley, and red pepper flakes to taste (if using). Cover and simmer for 10 minutes. Bring to a boil, then add the monkfish.

Bring the broth back to a boil and add the mussels and clams. When the shellfish begin to open, add the white fish and shrimp. Cook until the fish is cooked through, about 5 minutes.

Meanwhile, to make the croutons, heat the remaining 3 tablespoons olive oil in a medium skillet over medium heat. Add the bread cubes and cook, turning often, until the bread begins to crisp and brown.

To serve, ladle some shellfish, shrimp, and fish into each bowl. Pour some broth over the seafood and garnish with the croutons, scallions, and remaining 2 tablespoons parsley.

LASAGNA alla Mamma

Serves 8 to 10

Believe it or not, some claim that lasagna, one of the most beloved dishes in Italian cuisine, was created by the British, because the first cookbook believed to be published in Britain in the 14th century included a recipe similar to lasagna. I believe that the Romans brought the recipe to the British Isles during their conquests. Lasagna is thoroughly Italian.

We Italians know that lasagna was created in Naples during the Middle Ages. Italian immigrants brought their favorite variations to America beginning in the late 1800s.

Making lasagna is labor intensive, but it will feed a crowd. In most Italian-American families, including mine, lasagna is served on special occasions.

¼ cup olive oil

1 medium onion, minced

1 (28-ounce) can whole peeled San Marzano tomatoes or 10 Roma tomatoes

2 tablespoons shredded fresh basil or 4 whole basil leaves

½ teaspoon sea salt

1½ pounds lasagna pasta

1 (32-ounce) container ricotta cheese

1 pound mozzarella cheese, cut into ¼-inch slices

Preheat the oven to 375°F.

Heat the oil in large saucepan over low heat. Add the onion and tomatoes with their juices. (If using fresh tomatoes, see the preparation instructions on page 14.) Add the basil and salt. Simmer, stirring to break up the tomatoes, for 30 to 40 minutes.

Meanwhile, put a large pot of salted water on the stove to boil for the pasta. Cook the pasta until almost al dente, 8 to 10 minutes, then drain.

Lightly coat the bottom of an 8 x 12-inch baking dish with some of the tomato sauce. Arrange a layer of lasagna pasta, end to end, to cover the bottom completely.

Cover the pasta with a layer of ricotta. Add a ladle full of sauce on top. Place 6 slices of mozzarella, evenly spaced, over the sauce. Then begin the process again: pasta, ricotta, sauce, mozzarella. Add a last layer of pasta and mozzarella, then one more ladle full of sauce.

Cover the baking dish with aluminum foil and bake for 35 minutes. Remove the foil and bake for an additional 10 minutes.

PORCHETTA
Serves 8 to 12

Porchetta is the pièce de résistance *of any feast. This roast pork, which cooks for several hours, has remarkably crispy skin and succulent meat.*

Porchetta was a favorite of the Roman Emperor Nero and was served at Roman army camps, affording a nourishing meal to hungry soldiers, who did not get to eat meat often. The ancient Roman version of porchetta was roasted underground in a pit.

In the 15th century, Italy began to observe Sunday as a holy day. Making and enjoying porchetta became central to the day's activities.

When serving porchetta to your guests, make sure everyone gets a piece of the cracklings—the sublime crispy skin.

1 (7- to 8-pound) bone-in, skin-on pork shoulder roast or
    1 (6- to 7-pound) boneless roast, fat trimmed to ¼-inch thickness
3 tablespoons fennel seeds
1 tablespoon red pepper flakes
Grated zest of 1 lemon
2 tablespoons chopped fresh sage
2 tablespoons chopped fresh rosemary
4 garlic cloves, minced
1½ tablespoons sea salt
½ teaspoon freshly ground black pepper
¼ cup olive oil

Score the skin and fat all over the roast in a checkerboard pattern, about ⅓ inch deep. Do not cut into the meat.

In a food processor (a mini processor works best), combine the fennel seeds, red pepper flakes, lemon zest, sage, rosemary, garlic, salt, and black pepper. Pour in the oil and pulse until the ingredients form a paste. Rub the paste all over the roast. If using a boneless roast, tie with kitchen string every 2 inches.

Put the roast in a large bowl and cover with plastic wrap. Refrigerate for at least 6 hours or overnight.

Remove the roast from the refrigerator 1 to 2 hours before roasting.

Preheat the oven to 450°F.

Transfer the pork to a roasting pan and roast for 35 minutes.

Reduce the oven temperature to 325°F and continue to roast for 3 to 4 hours. The roast is done when an instant-read thermometer inserted into the thickest part reads 180°F. (Bone-in roasts take longer to cook than boneless ones.)

Transfer the pork to a cutting board and let the meat sit for 15 to 30 minutes before carving and serving.

Roasted Summer VEGETABLES

Serves 8

*R*oasting vegetables is an easy way to prepare a colorful side dish. Using high heat ensures that the outsides of the vegetables crisp while the insides stay tender.

You can use any combination of vegetables you like, or just a single vegetable. And in the winter you can do the same with broccoli, cauliflower, and Brussels sprouts.

We always like to make extra, because the vegetables make a delicious snack the next day.

3 bell peppers, preferably a mix of colors, seeded and cut into thin strips

2 medium carrots, peeled and cut into 2-inch spears

1 pound asparagus, trimmed and cut into 1-inch pieces

3 zucchini or yellow summer squashes, sliced lengthwise into ¼-inch-thick planks

2 small eggplants, sliced horizontally into ¼-inch-thick disks

8 ounces portobello mushrooms, cut into ¼-inch-thick slices

¼ cup olive oil

6 garlic cloves, minced

2 tablespoons chopped fresh oregano

2 tablespoons red pepper flakes (optional)

Sea salt

Freshly ground pepper

Preheat the oven to 450°F.

In a large bowl, combine all the vegetables. Add the olive oil, garlic, oregano, and red pepper flakes (if using). Toss well to coat the vegetables. Season with salt and pepper to taste.

Spread out the vegetables in a single layer on two rimmed baking sheets. Roast until tender and slightly seared, 45 minutes to 1 hour.

ZABAGLIONE with Strawberries and Blueberries

Serves 4 to 6

*A*t old-fashioned Italian restaurants in New York, the captain would make *zabaglione at your table. Those were the days. Served with fresh berries, zabaglione is a rich comfort food.*

6 large egg yolks
3 tablespoons sugar
½ cup Marsala or sweet sherry
1 pint fresh strawberries, sliced
1 pint blueberries

Bring an inch of water to a simmer in the bottom of a double boiler over medium heat.

In the top of the double boiler, whisk the egg yolks and sugar together by hand or with a hand-held mixer. While beating, stream in the Marsala. Place the top on the bottom of the double boiler. Continue to whisk gently until the mixture is tepid. Begin to whisk vigorously until the mixture is thick and foamy and triples in size, 5 to 6 minutes.

Put half of the strawberries in the bottoms of serving dishes or wine glasses and fill halfway with custard. Add more strawberries and fill with the remaining custard. Top with fresh blueberries.

Almond BISCOTTI

Makes 24 cookies

The word biscotti comes from the roots bis *and* cotto, *meaning twice baked, which will make sense once you see the recipe that follows.*

Biscotti dipped in espresso or sweet wine are delightful. These cookies also go well with Zabaglione (page 161).

Biscotti improve in flavor if baked one or two days ahead. Just store them in an airtight container at room temperature.

2 cups all-purpose flour

1 cup sugar

1 teaspoon baking powder

¼ teaspoon salt

8 tablespoons (1 stick) unsalted butter, chilled

3 large eggs

1 teaspoon vanilla extract

2 teaspoons almond extract

1 cup chopped almonds

Preheat the oven to 350°F. Lightly coat a rimmed baking sheet with nonstick cooking spray

In a large bowl, mix the flour, sugar, baking powder, and salt. With a pastry blender or two knives, add the cold butter to the dry ingredients and mix until it resembles fine crumbs.

Whisk the eggs in another large bowl and remove 1 tablespoon of the beaten egg to use for brushing the biscotti later. Add the vanilla and almond extracts, the almonds, and the flour mixture to the eggs. Mix well to form a dough.

With moistened hands, divide the dough in half and form two loaves on the prepared baking sheet. Use the reserved beaten egg to brush the tops and sides of the loaves.

Bake until lightly browned, about 25 minutes. Cool on the baking sheet for 10 to 15 minutes. Transfer the loaves to a cutting board and use a serrated knife to cut on the diagonal into ½-inch slices.

Arrange the biscotti, cut-side down, on a clean baking sheet, return to the oven, and bake until golden, about 15 minutes. Transfer the biscotti to a rack to cool completely.

Chocolate Chip BISCOTTI

*T*his is a chocolaty variation on the classic
recipe. Using chocolate chips and walnuts
or pecans is a deliciously rich alternative.
   *Follow the recipe for Almond Biscotti
(page 162), but replace the almond extract
and almonds with the following ingredients:*

6 ounces semisweet chocolate chips
1 cup coarsely chopped walnuts or pecans
Pinch ground cinnamon

SPAGHETTI Carbonara

Serves 6

Alternative

T he black pepper sprinkled on top of this classic pasta recipe was thought to resemble coal dust, which is why this pasta dish is called carbonara. This is essentially bacon and egg pasta—a great way to have breakfast for dinner!

1 tablespoon olive oil

6 ounces pancetta, cut into ¼-inch cubes

4 large eggs

1 cup heavy cream

½ cup grated Parmesan cheese, divided

½ cup grated Pecorino Romano cheese, divided

1 teaspoon coarsely ground black pepper

1 pound spaghetti

Put a large pot of salted water on the stove to boil for the pasta.

In a large skillet, heat the olive oil over medium heat. Add the pancetta and cook until lightly browned, 3 to 4 minutes.

In a large bowl, whisk the eggs and cream until blended. Stir in half of the cheeses and the pepper.

Cook the spaghetti until al dente, about 8 minutes. Drain the pasta and transfer it to the bowl with the egg-cream mixture. Toss to coat the pasta. Add the pancetta and pan drippings and toss again.

Grind more black pepper on top and serve, passing the remaining cheese.

NICE GUY
MEETS PUNDIT

And the Emmy goes to...

DEE DEE: We have done a lot of TV, both apart and together, though the together kind is much more fun. It is how we met, after all. I worked in politics for many years in several roles including TV host and pundit. I was honored to win an Emmy in 2014 for *Fresh Outlook,* a public affairs show that dealt with national and international issues in Washington DC, the country, and the world.

PAUL: My wife is a gifted and provocative political commentator—and she knows how to make a TV appearance that has impact. She has real talent for live TV. Though live TV is not a natural fit for me, I have been in a number of successful TV series and movies.

I credit an early TV role as the beginning of my tough guy persona. I had the title role in a show called *Bert D'Angelo/Superstar.* I played a tough detective who is transferred to San Francisco after spending a decade busting bad guys on the mean streets of New York. Bert D'Angelo is a maverick whose unorthodox methods unsettle his young partner and frustrate his boss. I must have been convincing, because the attitude stuck.

DEE DEE: Paul and I had fun doing *Grandfathered* together with John Stamos. I was a featured party girl, and Paul was a natural playing John's dad. I figured out very quickly that TV shows move much more quickly than movies.

PAUL: Recently, I did an episode of *The Goldbergs* playing Jeff Garlin's dad. George Segal plays Albert "Pops" Solomon on the show. I did my first movie with George. Carl Reiner directed us in *Where's Poppa?* Making that film was a great experience, and it remains one of my favorite movies. It was a good reunion!

DEE DEE: We were on *Criminal Minds: Beyond Borders* with Gary Sinise. Paul directed Gary in the television movie *That Championship Season* twenty years ago, so it was another reunion. Paul guest-starred as a powerful Italian doctor who was a serial killer. I got to play a detective, and they gave me a gun, which made me very happy. Paul is always in demand.

We like nothing more than a cozy night watching TV and enjoying the comfort food we prepare for at-home evenings. Sometimes friends join us to see a season finale, re-watch an old movie, or binge on a show we missed. On those casual nights, we set up a buffet and let our guests serve themselves.

> "We like nothing more than a cozy night watching TV and enjoying the comfort food we prepare for at-home evenings."
>
> —DEE DEE

Dee Dee's Special Cocktail

THE GOLDEN WINNER

Serves 1

I wanted this drink to be smooth and to go with everything, so I used golden rum—the same color as my Emmy. We serve the Golden Winner in a Champagne flute to make it more festive.

Here is a golden opportunity to feel like a winner—cheers!

3 ounces golden rum
2 ounces apricot juice
1 ounce orange juice
Orange peel

Fill a cocktail shaker halfway with ice. Add the rum, apricot juice, and orange juice. Cover and shake for 10 seconds. Strain into a Champagne flute. Garnish with an orange twist.

Menu

Dee Dee's Special Cocktail:
THE GOLDEN WINNER

Italian POPCORN
CAPONATA
PASTA e PISELLI
CHICKEN Scarpariello
Stuffed ZUCCHINI
CANNOLI Dessert Dip

ALTERNATIVE
LEEKS with Wine Sauce over Penne

Italian POPCORN

Serves 6

Nothing is cozier than watching TV while eating a freshly made bowl of popcorn. The cheese makes this recipe special.

¼ cup olive oil
12 cups freshly popped popcorn
1 cup grated Parmesan cheese
Sea salt

Put the popcorn in a large serving bowl and pour the olive oil over the top. Toss to coat. Sprinkle with the Parmesan cheese and mix well. Salt to taste.

PINOT, PASTA, AND PARTIES

CAPONATA
Serves 6

This Sicilian sweet and sour eggplant stew is a sensational appetizer, served with slices of toasted Italian bread. It's especially delicious with hardboiled eggs! Since eggplant is so absorbent, it is a good idea to make the caponata a day or two before you plan to serve it. Keep it covered in the refrigerator. That extra time will give the flavors a chance to meld. Caponata can be served warm, at room temperature, or cold.

5 tablespoons olive oil, divided
1 large eggplant, cut into ½-inch cubes
Sea salt
Freshly ground black pepper
1 cup coarsely chopped celery
2 cups coarsely chopped onion
1½ cups coarsely chopped fresh
    or canned tomatoes
¼ cup red wine vinegar

1 tablespoon sugar
3 tablespoons pine nuts
¼ cup capers
7 green pitted olives, sliced
¼ cup chopped fresh basil

Heat 3 tablespoons of the olive oil in a large skillet over high heat. Add the eggplant and season with salt and pepper. Cook, stirring often, until the eggplant is soft and starting to brown.

With a slotted spoon, transfer the eggplant to a plate. Add the remaining 2 tablespoons olive oil to the skillet and reduce the heat to medium. Add the celery and cook for 5 minutes. Add the onion and cook until beginning to brown. Add the tomatoes and season again with salt and pepper. Cover and cook for 7 minutes.

Return the eggplant to the skillet. Lower the heat to medium-low, cover, and simmer, stirring occasionally, for 8 minutes.

As the mixture is simmering, heat the vinegar in a small saucepan over medium-low heat. Stir in the sugar until dissolved. Add the pine nuts, capers, and olives and cook for 30 seconds. Transfer the contents of the saucepan to the simmering skillet. Cover and cook for 3 minutes. Stir in the fresh basil.

Transfer to a serving bowl.

PASTA e PISELLI
Serves 6 to 8

Pasta and peas is a traditional Neapolitan dish that was made in the spring when peas were in season. This recipe works very well with frozen peas, so we can have it year round. It is a very simple pasta—the best of Italian comfort food.

¼ cup olive oil
6 ounces pancetta
1 large onion
½ cup dry white wine
2 cups frozen peas
1 pound fettuccine
Sea salt
1½ cups grated Parmesan cheese

Put a large pot of salted water on the stove to boil for the pasta.

Heat the olive oil in a large skillet over medium-high heat. Add the pancetta and sauté until browned and crisp, 6 to 8 minutes. Use a slotted spoon to transfer the pancetta to paper towels to drain.

Add the onion to the skillet and sauté until translucent. Add the wine and reduce for 5 minutes.

Return the cooked pancetta to the skillet, add the frozen peas, and cook until heated through, about 5 minutes.

Meanwhile, cook the pasta according to the package instructions until al dente. Drain, reserving ½ cup of the pasta cooking water. Add the pasta to the skillet and toss to coat with the sauce. Add some of the reserved pasta cooking water if needed. Season with salt to taste.

Remove the skillet from the heat and toss the pasta with the Parmesan before serving.

CHICKEN Scarpariello

Serves 6

*T*his exceptional dish, which contains chicken, sausage, peppers, and potatoes, is thought to have evolved with Italian immigrants in the United States. Scarpariello *means "in the style of the shoemaker." No one knows if the name refers to the fact that it was a workingman's dinner or that the dish was "cobbled" together.*

This splendid main course improves if you make it a day ahead, which will leave you time the day of your dinner party to prepare other food.

1½ cups light olive oil

2 small chickens, each cut into 8 pieces

2 hot Italian sausage links

2 sweet Italian sausage links

1 large red bell pepper, seeded and cut into strips

1 large yellow bell pepper, seeded and cut into strips

3 garlic cloves, minced

2 or 3 small potatoes, peeled, boiled, and sliced (optional)

½ cup red wine vinegar

½ cup chicken broth

½ cup dry white wine

¼ teaspoon dried oregano

Sea salt

Freshly ground black pepper

Heat the oil in a large Dutch oven over medium-high heat. Cook the chicken, in batches, until brown, about 5 minutes on each side. Transfer the chicken to paper towels to absorb the excess oil.

Pierce the sausages a few times with a fork, then brown on all sides for about 5 minutes. Transfer the sausages to paper towels to absorb the excess oil. Cut into 1-inch slices if desired.

Add the bell peppers and garlic and sauté until they soften and begin to brown, about 5 minutes. Remove the vegetables with a slotted spoon and transfer to paper towels to absorb the excess oil.

Add the potatoes (if using), vinegar, chicken broth, wine, oregano, and salt and pepper to taste. Stir well. Cover and simmer until the chicken is cooked through, about 10 minutes. (If you wish, at this point you can remove the Dutch oven from the heat and set aside to cool. Refrigerate overnight. The next day, reheat over medium heat, covered, until heated through.) Uncover the pot, stir, and continue cooking until the sauce has reduced slightly, about 10 minutes.

Stuffed ZUCCHINI

Serves 6

This recipe uses two cheeses for which Calabria, located in the foot of the Italian boot, is known: Pecorino Romano and ricotta. The stuffing is speckled with tomato and mint. You can eat the zucchini straight from the oven or make the dish ahead and serve at room temperature.

6 medium zucchini (about 2 pounds total), halved lengthwise

7 tablespoons olive oil, divided

1 yellow onion, finely chopped

2 medium tomatoes, cored, seeded, and chopped

2 cups ricotta

¾ cup grated Pecorino Romano cheese, divided

¾ cup Homemade Bread Crumbs (page 38), divided

3 tablespoons chopped fresh flat-leaf parsley

2 teaspoons dried mint or 2 tablespoons chopped fresh mint

¼ teaspoon dried oregano

2 large egg yolks, beaten

Sea salt

Freshly ground black pepper

Using a small spoon, scoop out and discard the pulp from each zucchini half, leaving a ¼-inch-thick shell.

Heat 3 tablespoons of the olive oil in a 10-inch skillet over medium heat. Add the onion and sauté until the onion is translucent, about 6 minutes. Add the tomatoes and sauté until soft, about 4 more minutes. Remove the pan from the heat and set aside.

In a medium bowl, stir together the ricotta, ¼ cup of the Pecorino, ¼ cup of the bread crumbs, the parsley, mint, oregano, and egg yolks. Fold in the onion mixture and season with salt and pepper. Set the filling aside.

Place an oven rack about 7 inches from the broiler element and turn on the broiler. Line a rimmed baking sheet with aluminum foil.

Rub the insides of the zucchini with 2 tablespoons of olive oil and season lightly with salt. Place the zucchini, cut-side up, on the lined baking sheet and broil for 5 minutes.

Remove the baking sheet from the oven and fill each zucchini half with the ricotta mixture until it mounds slightly but does not spill over the edges of the zucchini.

Sprinkle each stuffed zucchini with the remaining Pecorino and bread crumbs. Drizzle the remaining olive oil on top.

Broil until the zucchini are soft and the tops are lightly browned, 10 to 15 minutes.

CANNOLI Dessert Dip

Serves 10

This recipe is a new twist on the popular Italian pastry, cannoli, which means little tubes. For this dessert, the creamy filling is used as a dip. This dessert is so flavorful, a little goes a long way!

2 cups ricotta cheese
1 (8-ounce) package cream cheese
1½ cup confectioners' sugar
1 teaspoon vanilla extract
1 cup miniature semisweet chocolate chips

Combine the ricotta cheese and cream cheese in a food processor.

Gradually add the sugar, then the vanilla, and mix until smooth. Transfer the mixture to a bowl.

Fold the chocolate chips into the cheese mixture. Cover the bowl with plastic wrap and refrigerate for at least 10 minutes.

Serve the cannoli dip in a bowl on a platter surrounded by broken cannoli shells, waffle cones, or pizzelles.

LEEKS with Wine Sauce over Penne

Serves 4

This is an elegant, light pasta that works well if you are serving a full, rich meal. It's a departure from red sauce and more typical Italian vegetables.

2 pounds medium leeks

¼ cup olive oil

½ cup dry white wine

1 teaspoon sea salt

½ teaspoon freshly ground black pepper

2 tablespoons minced fresh flat-leaf parsley leaves

1 pound penne

¼ cup grated Parmesan cheese

Put a large pot of salted water on the stove to boil for the pasta.

Trim and discard the dark green tops and outer leaves from the leeks. Trim a thin slice from the root end of the leeks and cut each leek in half lengthwise. Wash the trimmed leeks. Spread the inner layers gently to remove any trace of soil without separating the layers. If the leeks are very sandy, soak them a number of times in clean water.

Put the leeks, cut-side down, on a cutting board and slice crosswise into very thin strips.

Heat the oil in a large skillet over medium heat. Add the leeks and sauté until wilted, about 10 minutes. Reduce the heat if the leeks start to brown.

Add the wine, salt, and pepper, reduce the heat to low, and simmer until the sauce thickens a bit and the scent of wine fades, about 5 minutes. Stir in the parsley. Taste to see if additional salt and pepper are needed.

While the sauce is cooking, cook the penne according to the package instructions until al dente, then drain. Toss the hot pasta with the leek sauce in the skillet. Add the grated cheese and mix well.

Transfer to pasta bowls and serve immediately.

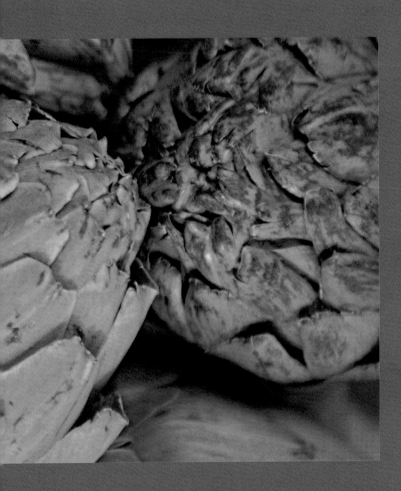

ART: A LIFELONG
LOVE AFFAIR

A True Renaissance Man

DEE DEE: Since Paul was a little boy, he's been drawing pictures, particularly of people. He has drawings that he made when he was eight or nine that look like the work of a mature artist. He loves to create things with his hands and in his mind and heart.

PAUL: When I was in my thirties, I wanted to figure out how I could study art. I audited some classes at the Art Students League in New York. I observed figure and architectural drawing and painting and found them too quiet. When I asked the receptionist where the sculpture department was, she pointed downstairs. I followed the sounds of hammering and clay being pounded. On the landing, I encountered a man whom I recognized as the renowned sculptor and instructor Jose de Creeft, whose beautiful bronze *Alice in Wonderland* sculpture can be found in Central Park.

I said to him, "Maestro, I'm a painter, but . . ." At the same moment we held our hands out as if we were each holding a nugget of gold. We said in unison "sculpture." I was in the right place.

I watched his classes making armatures, playing with clay, studying models for a bit, and immediately went back upstairs to enroll. I started working on a sculpture of a nude, but I had to leave to make a movie. It took me thirty years to get back into it.

At the age of sixty, I bought a book on bronze sculpting and dove in. Since then I have made more than twenty pieces of bronze, some life-size or larger and some as small as my hand.

DEE DEE: Our big project together was a commission for a bust of Jackie Robinson. Paul had three weeks to finish the sculpture, which was to be unveiled in Times Square. He couldn't seem to get it right. His first attempt looked like Burt Reynolds. The next was off, too. He was ready to give up.

"You can do this and you will," I said. "You can't let Jackie down." He finished at 2:00 in the morning. The statue was still warm when we sent it off the next day.

PAUL: Without Dee Dee's support, I never would have finished. She believes in me, and she's also tough!

I now look forward to creating a large bronze of Prince.

My interest in art goes far beyond mild participation. It has been a lifelong love affair. The only thing I love more is Dee Dee.

DEE DEE: When Paul finishes a piece and when a sculpture is installed, we take our celebration of the event seriously. We always choose Paul's favorite foods. Sometimes we celebrate alone with a romantic dinner and sometimes we host a party for good friends.

Dee Dee's Special Cocktail

THE GREEN WITCH

Serves 1

Absinthe was a very popular spirit with artists at the end of the nineteenth century and beginning of the twentieth. It was called the "green fairy" by many, because of its vibrant color. Green is my favorite color—my wedding ring even has emeralds.

Absinthe has a very high alcohol content and was believed to cause hallucinations. Many illustrious artists were associated with absinthe, from Van Gogh to Poe, from Manet to Wilde, from Hemingway to Picasso.

Absinthe was outlawed for many years, and it just became legal in America again in 2007. I tried absinthe in New Orleans at the famous Old Absinthe House. I fell for the green elixir and have imbibed ever since.

I like drinking absinthe the traditional way, through a sugar cube, but this is a brighter, lighter twist to the green drink.

We sometimes add dry ice to make this drink a real witch's brew. Enjoy the potent potion!

2 ounces gin	½ ounce fresh lime juice
1 ounce absinthe	1 maraschino cherry
1 ounce Midori	Fresh mint leaves
½ ounce Green Chartreuse	Dry ice (optional)

Fill a cocktail shaker halfway with ice. Add the gin, absinthe, Midori, Green Chartreuse, and lime juice. Shake vigorously for 10 seconds. Strain into a martini glass. Garnish with a cherry and some mint leaves. If you wish, add dry ice for a special effect.

Menu

Dee Dee's Special Cocktail:

THE GREEN WITCH

Stuffed ARTICHOKES

PASTA alla Norma

Roasted POTATOES

OSSOBUCO

PANZANELLA

TIRAMISU

ALTERNATIVE

SCALLOPS with Bacon over Spinach

Stuffed ARTICHOKES
Serves 4

Stuffed artichokes look great on a platter. They are so much fun to eat leaf by leaf. Then you get down to the choke, remove it, and find the heart.

4 medium artichokes
2 cups seasoned Italian bread crumbs
3 tablespoons Pecorino Romano cheese
3 tablespoons chopped fresh flat-leaf parsley
2 garlic cloves, minced
Sea salt
Freshly ground black
6 tablespoons olive oil, plus more for drizzling
4 lemon slices

Preheat the oven to 375°F.

Wash the artichokes. Tug the leaves outward to loosen them up for stuffing. Trim the stems from the bottom of the artichokes so that they can stand. Trim off the tip of each leaf.

In a large bowl, mix the bread crumbs, cheese, parsley, garlic, and salt and pepper to taste. Gradually add the olive oil just until it is moist enough to stick together. You may not need all the oil.

Stuff the bread crumb mixture between the leaves of each artichoke. Start at the bottom and work your way around. Shake off any excess mixture.

Place the artichokes in a large baking pan and pour in ½ to 1 inch of water.

Drizzle olive oil over the stuffed artichokes. Place a lemon slice on top of each artichoke. Cover the pan tightly with aluminum foil.

Bake until a leaf pulls off easily, 60 to 80 minutes. Cool for 10 minutes before serving.

PASTA alla Norma

Serves 6 to 8

Pasta alla Norma is one of the best-loved Sicilian dishes. It was so popular in 19th-century Italy that it was named after Sicilian composer Bellini's very successful opera Norma. A marriage of delicious food and great opera is a dish made in heaven as far as I'm concerned.

2 large eggplants, cut into ¾-inch cubes
2 tablespoons kosher salt
4 tablespoons olive oil, divided
3 garlic cloves, minced
2 (28-ounce) cans crushed
    San Marzano tomatoes
1 teaspoon red pepper flakes

¼ teaspoon dried oregano
Sea salt
1 pound rigatoni
1 cup chopped fresh basil
½ cup grated Parmesan cheese
1 cup whole-milk ricotta cheese
1 cup ricotta salata, grated

Put a large pot of salted water on the stove to boil for the pasta.

Preheat the oven to 400°F.

In a colander, toss the eggplant and the kosher salt. Set the colander in the sink and let the eggplant drain for 1 hour. Rinse the eggplant and pat dry with paper towels.

Coat a rimmed baking sheet with 2 tablespoons of the olive oil. Put the eggplant on the baking sheet and toss to coat with the oil. Spread the eggplant out in an even layer. Bake until the eggplant is browned and tender, about 25 minutes. For even cooking, stir the eggplant and turn the baking sheet once or twice during baking.

In a large skillet, heat the remaining 2 tablespoons olive oil over medium heat. Add the garlic and sauté until golden, about 3 minutes. Add the crushed tomatoes, red pepper flakes, oregano, and sea salt to taste. Bring to a boil, then reduce the heat and simmer for 10 minutes.

While the sauce is cooking, cook the rigatoni until al dente, 10 to 12 minutes. Drain the pasta and return it to the pot over low heat.

Add half of the sauce and mix well. Then add half of the eggplant, half of the basil, and the grated Parmesan cheese and toss to combine. Remove from the heat and gently stir in the ricotta.

Transfer the pasta to a platter or individual plates. Top with the remaining eggplant, sauce, basil, and the ricotta salata and serve.

Roasted POTATOES

Serves 6

Roasted potatoes are always a great side dish for meat or poultry. Crispy on the outside, creamy on the inside is how we like them. This simple recipe never disappoints.

2 pounds fingerlings, small red new potatoes, Yukon gold potatoes, or a mixture
¼ cup olive oil
3 tablespoons dried rosemary
Sea salt
Freshly ground pepper

Preheat the oven to 400°F.

Cut the potatoes in half or in quarters so you end up with 1½-inch pieces.

Put the potatoes in a zip-top plastic bag and add the olive oil, rosemary, and salt and pepper to taste. Shake until the potatoes are well coated.

Spread the potatoes in a single, uncrowded layer on a rimmed baking sheet. Roast until the potatoes are browned and crispy, about 1 hour. Turn the potatoes once or twice to ensure even browning.

Remove from the oven, season with more salt and pepper, and serve.

OSSOBUCO

Serves 4 to 6

Ossobuco is a veal dish from Milan. Its name translates to "bone with a hole," referring to the marrow hole visible when a veal shank is cross cut. This is a humble farmer's stew, but the flavor is fit for a nobleman. The veal is so succulent it falls off the bone.

FOR THE VEAL:

6 (3-inch-thick) veal shanks

All-purpose flour, for dredging

3 tablespoons olive oil

2 garlic cloves, minced

½ cup chopped carrot

1 tablespoon chopped fresh basil

Sea salt

Freshly ground black pepper

1 cup dry white wine

2 cups diced fresh or canned tomatoes

2 tablespoons unsalted butter

FOR THE GREMOLATA:

2 tablespoons chopped fresh flat-leaf parsley

1 garlic clove, minced

½ teaspoon dried sage

Grated zest of 1 lemon rind

Preheat the oven to 400°F.

Dredge the veal in flour. Heat the olive oil in a large Dutch oven (or an oven-safe skillet with a lid) over medium heat. Add the veal and cook, turning the shanks as they begin to brown. Add the garlic and cook until the shanks are well seared and the garlic browns.

Add the carrot, basil, and salt and pepper to taste and cook until the onion softens. Add the wine, cover, and lower the heat. Simmer, stirring often, for 10 minutes.

Add the tomatoes and butter, cover, and continue to simmer for 3 more minutes.

Place the covered Dutch oven in the oven and cook for 30 minutes. Lower the oven temperature to 350°F and cook for an additional 30 minutes.

Prepare the gremolata while the veal is braising. Mix the parsley, garlic, sage, and lemon zest.

When the braising time is up, remove the Dutch oven from the oven and sprinkle the gremolata over the meat. Cover and return to the oven for 10 more minutes.

PANZANELLA
Serves 6

This traditional bread salad is colorful and provides a great use for leftover bread. The dry bread becomes moist again when it absorbs the dressing. We suggest using a variety of tomatoes. Heirlooms are especially beautiful, and they taste good, too.

6 ounces string beans, trimmed

2 or 3 thick slices crusty bread

¼ cup olive oil, plus more for brushing

1 pint cherry tomatoes, halved, or 2 large tomatoes,
    coarsely chopped, or a mixture

½ red onion, thinly sliced

5 large basil leaves, torn

¼ cup red wine vinegar

Sea salt

Freshly ground black pepper

Preheat an outdoor grill or broiler.

Blanch the string beans in a large saucepan of boiling water until just tender, about 5 minutes. Drain and let cool.

Brush both sides of the bread slices lightly with olive oil. Grill or broil the bread, turning once, until just starting to char, about 3 minutes. Cut the grilled bread into 1-inch cubes.

In a serving bowl, toss the bread cubes with string beans, tomatoes, red onion, and basil.

Whisk together the oil and vinegar and season with salt and pepper. Pour the dressing over the salad. Toss thoroughly so the bread can absorb the dressing.

TIRAMISU

Serves 6 to 8

Tiramisu, which means pick me up or cheer me up in Italian, is a newcomer to Italian cuisine. It is said to have been invented in Venice in the 1960s. What a great addition to Italian desserts!

6 large egg yolks, at room temperature

½ cup sugar, divided

1 pound mascarpone

2 ounces dark rum or Kahlúa (optional)

4 large egg whites

24 ladyfingers

1½ cups espresso or ¾ cup strong American coffee + ¾ cup espresso

Unsweetened cocoa powder, for garnish

In a large bowl, whisk the egg yolks and ¼ cup of the sugar until the mixture has doubled in volume, 3 to 5 minutes. Add the mascarpone in two or three portions and whisk to combine. Add the rum or Kahlúa (if using) and continue whisking.

In another bowl, whip the egg whites and the remaining ¼ cup sugar until soft peaks form. Fold the egg whites into the mascarpone mixture in two or three portions.

Soak each ladyfinger in the espresso and arrange half of them tightly in the bottom of a 9-inch square baking dish or a similar-size oblong dish. Spread half of the mascarpone mixture on top of the ladyfingers. Top with the remaining ladyfingers and another layer of mascarpone.

Cover and refrigerate for 1 hour or up to 2 days to set the cream. Dust with cocoa before serving.

SCALLOPS with Bacon over Spinach

Alternative

Serves 4

This is our main course take on everyone's favorite hors d'oeuvres, scallops wrapped in bacon. The flavors come from the fresh seafood and the bacon and they don't need any extra help!

2 tablespoons olive oil
8 ounces bacon
1 pound sea scallops
1 pound spinach

In a large skillet, heat the olive oil over medium heat. Add the bacon. When the bacon is partially cooked, move it to one side of the pan and add the scallops. Sauté the scallops and bacon together until the bacon is crisp and the scallops are browned on both sides, about 7-10 minutes.

While the bacon and scallops are cooking, put the spinach in a large pot with 2 cups cold water. Cover and steam the spinach until wilted. Drain the spinach in a colander, pressing down on it with a large spoon to remove all the water.

Transfer the spinach to a large platter, add the scallops and bacon, and serve.

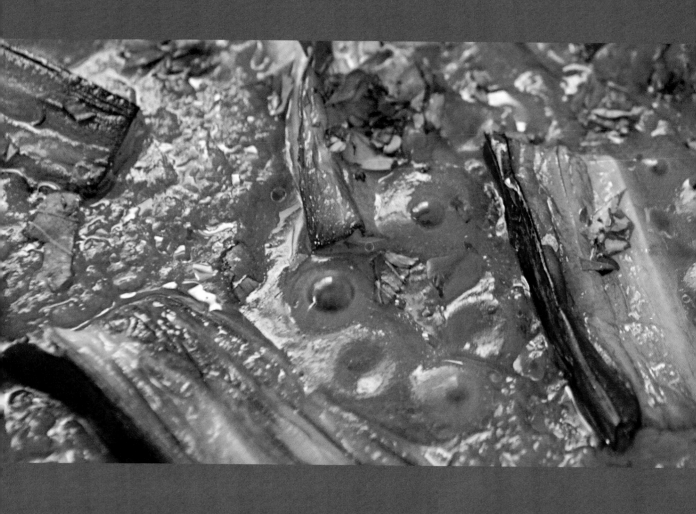

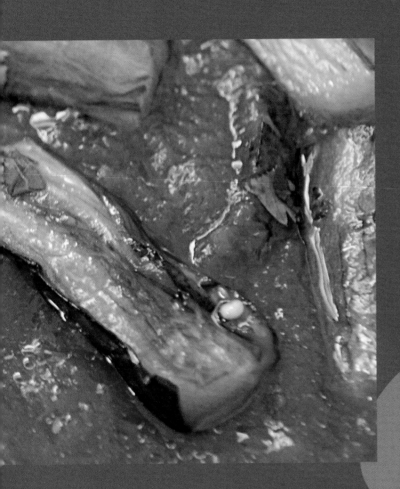

PATRIOTISM AT PLAY

Political Partying

DEE DEE: There is no contest that I am the more political one of our duo.

PAUL: Dee Dee is a strategic thinker. She is a specialist who is focused and concentrates. She is a force of nature who gets things done. I'm more of a reader, a studier, an artist with a capacious worldview. Rather than causing conflicts, our differences enrich our view of the world—well, most of the time. We know how lucky we are to have each other.

DEE DEE: I have worked on many campaigns—up to the presidential level. I have been elected as young republican national federation chairman, Indiana national committeewoman, and to a town council in Indiana, so I have been involved in politics in many ways and levels. I made the move from Indiana politics to the national scene. Though I love politics, I love my husband more. Instead of politics being my mission, my mission is enjoying life with Paul and the campaign is Pinot, pasta, and parties.

PAUL: I don't get involved in politics unless I am helping a friend or feel strongly about a mainstream issue. We do use our energy and influence to support candidates and issues that matter to us. We feel we all have to work to have our voices heard in this democracy of ours.

DEE DEE: We all have a responsibility to be politically active. That involves a lot more than going to the polls to vote. Be aware of what is going at the local, state, and national levels. Contribute to your party, favorite candidates, and organizations representing issues that concern you. And I mean more than money. Stand up for what you believe in. Volunteer your time to work to keep our country the best version of democracy imaginable. There is so much you can do to make our country even better.

The menu for this chapter is what we might serve for an informal fund-raiser or a strategy session.

> "Though I love politics, I love my husband more. Instead of politics being my mission, my mission is enjoying life with Paul and the campaign is Pinot, pasta, and parties."
>
> —DEE DEE

Dee Dee's Special Cocktail
THE MUSKET BALL
Serves 1

Politics means the business of the people. I wanted to honor our Revolutionary War heroes and founding fathers with bourbon.

In 1964 congress declared bourbon "America's Native spirit" so of course it's made in the USA and mostly in my birth state of Kentucky. We Kentuckians love our Bourbon especially in mint juleps during the derby, but I have created another great bourbon cocktail to enjoy and raise our spirits.

This drink would certainly be a favorite of congressional and White House staff—and perhaps even a few Supreme Court justices. It's a revolutionary drink for all Americans—Republicans, Democrats, and Independents.

2½ ounces bourbon
1 ounce Borghetti Caffè Sport espresso liqueur
½ ounce Aperol
Large ice ball
Orange peel

Fill a cocktail shaker halfway with ice. Add the bourbon, espresso liqueur, and Aperol. Cover and shake for 5 seconds. Strain into a rocks glass with a large ice ball. Garnish with a thumb-size piece of orange peel.

Menu

Dee Dee's Special Cocktail:
THE MUSKET BALL

CANNELLINI BEAN DIP
with Carrot Chips

Salumeria PIZZA

Northern CHICKEN CACCIATORE
with Mushrooms

Fennel and Blood Orange SALAD

Olive Oil CAKE

ALTERNATIVES

Southern CHICKEN CACCIATORE

Potato FRITTATA

CANNELLINI BEAN DIP with Carrot Chips

Makes about 2 cups

T*his healthy dip is packed with flavor—Mediterranean all the way. The crunch of the carrots complements the creaminess of the dip. For more variety, you can serve a crudité basket with an assortment of your favorite raw vegetables.*

1 (15-ounce) can cannellini beans, rinsed and drained

¼ cup extra-virgin olive oil, plus more for drizzling

1 head garlic, roasted (see page 128)

1 teaspoon dried rosemary

½ teaspoon cayenne pepper (optional)

Sea salt

4 large carrots, peeled and thinly sliced on a long diagonal

In a food processor, combine the beans, olive oil, roasted garlic, rosemary, cayenne pepper (if using), and salt to taste. Blend until the mixture is smooth.

Transfer the dip to a small serving bowl and drizzle some extra-virgin olive oil on top. Place the bowl in the center of a platter or cutting board and serve with the carrot chips.

Salumeria PIZZA

Serves 4

A n antipasto salad on a golden crust! This satisfying pizza does double duty. You can use any of your favorite Italian cured meats on this pie.

1 recipe Paul's Pizza Dough (page 36)
All-purpose flour, for dusting
¾ cup Marinara Sauce (page 14)
2 tablespoons grated Parmesan cheese
¼ teaspoon cracked black pepper
⅛ teaspoon red pepper flakes
Cayenne pepper
Fresh mozzarella, sliced
Salami, thinly sliced
Pepperoni, thinly sliced
Fresh basil leaves, cut into ribbons
Grape tomatoes, halved
2 beefsteak tomatoes, sliced
Cornmeal, for dusting

If you have a pizza stone, place it in the oven. Preheat the oven to 450°F.

Roll out the pizza dough on a well-floured work surface.

In a small bowl, combine the marinara sauce, Parmesan cheese, cracked black pepper, red pepper flakes, and a pinch of cayenne pepper. Stir well.

Spread the sauce on the dough, leaving a ½-inch border. Arrange the sliced mozzarella on the dough, then place the salami, pepperoni, basil, and tomatoes on top.

Sprinkle the preheated pizza stone or a baking sheet with cornmeal to keep the crust from sticking. Transfer the pizza to the stone or baking sheet. Bake until the crust is golden, about 15 minutes.

Northern CHICKEN CACCIATORE with Mushrooms
Serves 4

Chicken cacciatore translates to hunter's chicken, a way of preparing chicken that dates back to the Renaissance. The dish is a stew that has many variations. In the United States, chicken cacciatore is almost always made with tomato sauce, but in Italy that is not the case. In southern Italy, chicken cacciatore is usually made with red wine, and in the North white wine. This recipe is for a "white" chicken cacciatore, which looks a lot like chicken in wine sauce.

1 (3- to 4-pound) chicken, cut into 8 pieces

Sea salt

Freshly ground black pepper

All-purpose flour, for dusting

2 tablespoons olive oil

1 cup dry white wine

1 cup chicken stock or canned broth, divided

2 tablespoons unsalted butter

1 small onion, finely chopped

8 ounces pancetta, diced

1 pound assorted mushrooms, sliced

1 teaspoon dried thyme

Season the chicken pieces with salt and pepper. Dust the chicken with flour.

Heat the olive oil in a large skillet over medium-high heat. Add the chicken, in batches if necessary, and cook until lightly browned on all sides, about 5 minutes. Transfer the chicken to a plate and drain off all the oil from the skillet. Return the chicken to the skillet.

Add the white wine and ½ cup of the chicken stock. Cover and simmer until the chicken is tender, about 25 minutes.

While the chicken is cooking, melt the butter in another large skillet over medium heat. Add the onion and pancetta and cook, stirring, until the onion is soft, about 3 minutes. Add the mushrooms and cook for 3 minutes. Add the remaining ½ cup chicken stock and the thyme and cook for 5 minutes.

After the chicken has cooked for 25 minutes, add the mushroom mixture and any pan juices. Simmer for 2 minutes to blend the flavors. Season with additional salt and pepper.

Fennel and Blood Orange SALAD

Serves 6 to 8

This refreshing salad takes no time to prepare. The combination of fennel and oranges is unexpected and very tasty.

2 medium fennel bulbs

6 Blood oranges

Romaine lettuce leaves, torn into pieces

Extra-virgin olive oil

Sea salt

Freshly ground black pepper

1 tablespoon chopped fresh mint

Remove the tough outer layers of the fennel bulbs and trim any bruises or discolorations. Cut the bulbs in half lengthwise. Cut out the core at the base of each bulb. Cut the bulb lengthwise to make julienne strips.

Peel the oranges and remove all the white pith. Cut the oranges into bite-size chunks.

Combine the lettuce, fennel, and oranges on a platter. Drizzle with olive oil, season with salt and pepper to taste, and toss with the chopped mint.

Olive Oil CAKE

Serves 8 to 12

*S*ome of the best olive oils in the world come from Italy. As you can see from this recipe, olive oil is even used for baking. This is a moist, rich, not too sweet cake with a hint of lemon. Italians eat this cake at breakfast, too. We like to serve it dusted with powdered sugar and topped with fresh raspberries.

Unsalted butter, for greasing the pan
All-purpose flour, for dusting the pan
1½ cups cake flour
1 teaspoon baking soda
½ teaspoon baking powder
¼ teaspoon salt
2 large eggs
4 large egg yolks
1½ cups sugar

1 cup buttermilk
½ cup milk
¾ cup olive oil
Grated zest of 1 lemon
¼ cup fresh lemon juice
Confectioners' sugar, for dusting

Preheat the oven to 350°F. Butter and flour a 9 x 5-inch loaf pan, shaking out the excess flour.

Mix the cake flour, baking soda, baking powder, and salt in a medium bowl.

In a large bowl, whip the whole eggs and eggs yolks together, then gradually add the sugar. Add the buttermilk and milk.

While whipping on high speed, add the olive oil in a very slow drizzle until smooth. Lower the mixer speed and slowly add the dry mixture, mixing until just combined. Mix in the lemon zest, and lemon juice, then pour the batter into the prepared loaf pan.

Bake until the top is golden brown and a toothpick inserted into the center comes out clean, about 1 hour.

Let the cake cool completely before removing it from the pan. Transfer the cake to a plate for serving. Dust the top with confectioners' sugar and serve plain, or add fresh berries or your favorite gelato to make it extra special.

Southern CHICKEN CACCIATORE

Serves 6

This recipe for chicken cacciatore is from southern Italy and uses tomatoes. This is the version most commonly served in the United States.

1 (3- to 4-pound) chicken, cut into 8 pieces
1 teaspoon dried oregano
Sea salt
Freshly ground black pepper
¼ cup olive oil
1 yellow bell pepper, seeded and diced
1 red bell pepper, seeded and diced
2 small carrots, peeled and sliced
5 garlic cloves, minced
½ teaspoon dried rosemary or
   1 tablespoon fresh rosemary

½ teaspoon dried thyme or
   1 tablespoon fresh thyme
1 cup dry red wine
1 cup chicken stock or canned broth
1 (28-ounce) can crushed
   San Marzano tomatoes
1 pound assorted mushrooms, sliced
1 cup pitted Kalamata olives
⅓ cup chopped fresh flat-leaf parsley

Preheat the oven to 375°F.

Season the chicken pieces with the oregano and salt and pepper to taste.

Heat the olive oil in a large Dutch oven over medium-high heat. Add the chicken, in batches if necessary, and cook until lightly browned on all sides, about 5 minutes. Transfer the chicken to a plate.

Add the bell peppers, carrots, garlic, rosemary, and thyme to the oil remaining in the Dutch oven and sauté for 5 minutes. Add the wine and reduce it for 5 minutes.

Add the chicken stock and tomatoes. Season with salt and pepper to taste.

Return the chicken to the Dutch oven and cover with the sauce. Bring to a simmer. Cover the Dutch oven. Transfer it to the oven and cook for 50 minutes. Remove the lid and add the mushrooms. Cook, uncovered, until the sauce has thickened and the chicken is falling off the bone, about 20 minutes.

Garnish with the olives and parsley.

Potato FRITTATA

Alternative

Serves 4 to 6

A frittata is wonderful for entertaining, because you can make it well before your guests are expected and serve it warm or at room temperature. We serve frittatas for brunch or lunch, with a salad and good bread on the side. You can put anything in a frittata. Think of it as an omelet that you bake. Leftovers are great eaten cold, but you are not likely to have any. Growing up we called this potatoes and eggs—a staple of every Italian kitchen!

2 tablespoons olive oil

2 pounds Yukon Gold potatoes, sliced

8 large eggs

2 cups milk

2 tablespoons grated Parmesan cheese

½ cup chopped fresh flat-leaf parsley

7 tablespoons unsalted butter

Sea salt

Freshly ground black pepper

Preheat the oven to 350°F.

In a large oven-safe skillet, warm the olive oil over medium heat. Add the potatoes and sauté until golden brown, 12 to 15 minutes. Transfer the potatoes to a paper towel to drain and cool.

Whisk the eggs, milk, cheese, and parsley in a bowl until fluffy. Stir the potatoes into the mixture until they are completely coated.

In the same skillet, melt the butter over medium heat. Add the egg and potato mixture. Cook without stirring until the bottom of the frittata is firm.

Transfer the skillet to the oven and cook until golden brown on top and set in the middle, 20 to 30 minutes.

Allow the frittata to sit for at least 5 minutes. Serve directly from the skillet while warm or at room temperature. Add salt and pepper to taste.

SHINE ON THE
RUNWAY OF LIFE

A Table with Personal Style

DEE DEE: Dressing a plate with sumptuous food and putting yourself together require a similar approach. Having a sense of style that is true to who you are goes a long way to boosting your appeal and making you happy.

Paul is the traditionalist and I am the adventurer. Just as he is a steady, strong cook, he is conservative about fashion. He wears elegant handmade suits, and I throw together whatever I like.

PAUL: You can say that again! Dee Dee had the confidence to wear a $49.99 sequin camouflage mini-dress to the *Vanity Fair* Oscar party because she wanted *American Sniper* to win at the Oscars that year. She could have had any dress she wanted, but that was the only one for her! She looked terrific.

DEE DEE: It takes flair to have memorable parties. From the menu to the guest list, from the flowers to the table settings, orchestrating a fun event takes planning. The atmosphere you create adds to the charm of a party. Even if you are planning a casual meal, aesthetics do matter. Your guests will respond to the environment you fashion.

I like to have themed parties which makes the decor, dishes, food all come together whether it's movies, TV, fashion, politics, or music. Themes are fun and helpful in planning parties. I love a vibrant table and collect serving bowls, spoons, forks, platters, and napkins so that I can change it up easily. Plain white plates show off your food, and you can buy them anywhere. I have stacks of them for buffets. You can go for a pristine look—all white with white napkins and white flowers or add contrast with bright, textured napkins and bursts of color in flowers around the house.

Sometimes the dishes on my table match, and sometimes I mix them up—different plates for each course or even different plates within a course. You can find so many inexpensive things for the table at flea markets, consignment shops, and home goods stores. The vintage linens, glasses, antique platters, hand-painted porcelain dessert plates, pottery of all sorts, imported table wear, and great vases you find on your treasure hunts will add a distinctive note to your table.

Make it fun so that you can shine at your own party. The more you entertain, the easier it becomes.

"Make it fun so that you can shine at your own party. The more you entertain, the easier it becomes."

—DEE DEE

Dee Dee's Special Cocktail
THE VENUS
Serves 1

When you entertain with style, you are showing love and respect for your guests. Since Paul and I are a love match in the kitchen and in every way. I dedicate this cocktail to the goddess of love.

2 ounces vodka
1 ounce ginger liqueur
1 ounce pear juice
¼ ounce fresh lemon juice
¼ ounce simple syrup
Lemon wedge, for garnish
Candied ginger, for garnish

Fill a cocktail shaker halfway with ice. Add the vodka, ginger liqueur, pear juice, lemon juice, and simple syrup. Cover and shake for 5 seconds. Strain into a martini glass filled with ice. Garnish with the lemon wedge and candied ginger.

Menu

Dee Dee's Special Cocktail:
THE VENUS

GRILLED FIGS with Goat Cheese
and Balsamic Glaze

BAGNA CAUDA

Italian Kale SALAD

FARFALLE with Asparagus,
Mushrooms, and Pancetta

VEAL Piccata

Poached PEACHES
with Raspberry Sauce

GRILLED FIGS with Goat Cheese and Balsamic Glaze

Serves 8

This appetizer not only presents very well, but it also has a sophisticated blend of flavors. You can use either your broiler or an outdoor grill to cook the figs.

1 cup balsamic vinegar
16 ripe figs
4 ounces goat cheese, at room temperature
¼ cup shelled pistachios or chopped walnuts

Heat the balsamic vinegar in a small saucepan over medium heat until it simmers. Reduce the heat to low and let the vinegar simmer until it starts to thicken, 10 to 15 minutes. Turn off the heat and transfer the vinegar to a small bowl to cool.

Prepare each fig by cutting off the stem and then making two slits from the top of the fig to three-quarters of the way down in the shape of an X. This creates a pocket in the middle of the fig. Stuff each fig with about a teaspoon of goat cheese.

If broiling: Preheat the broiler. Place the figs on a rimmed baking sheet and broil until the cheese starts to bubble and brown, about 5 minutes.

If grilling: Preheat the grill over medium heat. Lightly brush the stuffed figs with olive oil and place them on the grill. Cover and grill until the figs soften and brown slightly and the cheese bubbles.

Transfer the figs to a serving tray. Sprinkle the nuts on top and drizzle with the balsamic glaze.

BAGNA CAUDA
Serves 6

B*agna cauda is a hot dip, the Italian version of a vegetable fondue. A big basket of colorful vegetables makes this a spectacular appetizer. Use slices of bread to catch the dip that drips from the vegetables.*

1 cup olive oil

4 tablespoons unsalted butter, at room temperature

6 anchovy fillets

4 garlic cloves, chopped

Sea salt

Freshly ground black pepper

1 loaf crusty Italian bread, sliced, or bread sticks

Assorted vegetables for dipping (use any combination):

3 large carrots, peeled and cut into spears

4 celery stalks, cut into 3-inch sticks

1 fennel bulb, cut into 1-inch strips

1 large red bell pepper, seeded and cut into 1-inch strips

1 large yellow pepper, seeded and cut into 1-inch strips

Leaves from 1 head Belgian endive

1 pound asparagus spears, trimmed and blanched

Florets from 1 small head broccoli, blanched

Florets from 1 small head cauliflower, blanched

Blend the oil, butter, anchovies, and garlic in a food processor or blender until smooth. Transfer the mixture to a medium saucepan. Cook over low heat for 15 minutes, stirring occasionally. The sauce will separate. Season with salt and pepper to taste.

Pour the sauce into a fondue pot, chafing dish, or other flameproof casserole. Set the pot over an alcohol burner or a gas table burner to keep warm. Serve with bread and your choice of vegetables for dipping.

Italian Kale SALAD

Serves 4 to 6

T*hough kale has become ubiquitous here recently, Italians have been eating greens for centuries. It's one of the reasons the Mediterranean diet is so healthy. The trick to this salad is to cut the kale into thin strips.*

1 bunch kale, tough stems removed and leaves cut into ribbons

1 large tomato, seeded and diced

½ cup canned chickpeas, rinsed and drained

¼ cup chopped red onion

⅓ cup shaved Parmesan or Pecorino Romano cheese, plus more for serving

1 teaspoon Dijon mustard

2 tablespoons fresh lemon juice

1 teaspoon honey

Sea salt

Freshly ground black pepper

¼ cup extra-virgin olive oil, plus more for drizzling

¼ cup Homemade Bread Crumbs (page 38)

Combine the kale, tomato, chickpeas, red onion, and cheese in a salad bowl.

In a small bowl, whisk together the mustard, lemon juice, honey, and salt and pepper to taste. Add the olive oil in a steady stream while continuing to whisk. Add more salt and pepper if needed. Pour the dressing sparingly over the salad and toss to coat.

Serve the salad topped with bread crumbs, grated cheese, and a drizzle of olive oil.

FARFALLE with Asparagus, Mushrooms, and Pancetta

Serves 4 to 6

In the United States, this pasta shape is known as bowties, but in Italian farfalle means butterflies. The combination of fresh sautéed vegetables and light, creamy sauce creates a simple, tasty main course or side dish.

3 (½-inch-thick) slices pancetta,
  cut into thin strips
4 tablespoons olive oil, divided
2 garlic cloves, minced
10 ounces assorted mushrooms, sliced
Sea salt
Freshly ground black pepper

1 pound asparagus, trimmed and
  cut into 1-inch pieces
1 cup heavy cream
1 cup fresh basil leaves, shredded
1 pound farfalle
¼ cup grated Parmesan cheese,
  plus more for serving

Put a large pot of salted water on the stove to boil for the pasta. Put a medium pot of salted water on the stove to boil for the asparagus.

Cook the pancetta in a small skillet over medium heat until crisp. Drain the pancetta on paper towels.

In a medium saucepan, heat 3 tablespoons of the olive oil over medium-low heat. Add the garlic and sauté until soft. Add the sliced mushrooms and season with salt and pepper to taste. Sauté for 10 minutes.

Meanwhile, cook the asparagus in the medium pot of boiling water just until tender, 3 to 4 minutes. Do not overcook, since the asparagus will be cooked again in the sauce. Add the asparagus to the mushrooms.

Cook the farfalle in the large pot of boiling water until al dente, 10 to 15 minutes. Drain.

While the pasta is cooking, pour the cream into the pan with the mushrooms and reduce over high heat until the sauce is thickened. Add the pancetta and basil and toss. Taste and add more salt and pepper if needed.

Transfer the pasta to a heated bowl and toss with the remaining 1 tablespoon olive oil. Add the sauce, vegetables, and grated Parmesan and toss. Serve immediately, passing a bowl of grated Parmesan for topping.

VEAL Piccata

Serves 4

*I*talians have a way with veal, and veal piccata is an elegant dish that you can make in a flash. The secret to making veal cutlets that melt in your mouth is to pound them very thin before cooking. This is one of our favorite main courses.

¼ cup all-purpose flour
Sea salt
Freshly ground black pepper
4 veal cutlets, pounded to ¼ inch thick
¼ cup olive oil
2 garlic cloves, minced
½ cup dry white wine
3 tablespoons fresh lemon juice
2 tablespoons salt-packed capers, soaked in water for 20 minutes, drained, and rinsed
2 tablespoons unsalted butter
1 tablespoon chopped fresh flat-leaf parsley
Lemon slices, for garnish

Put the flour in a flat dish and season with salt and pepper. Dredge the veal cutlets in the flour and shake off the excess.

Heat the olive oil in a large skillet over medium heat. Sauté the veal cutlets until golden, about 2 minutes per side. Transfer to a plate.

Add the garlic to the pan and sauté for 1 minute. Add the wine, lemon juice, and capers and bring the mixture to a boil. Scrape up the brown bits at the bottom of the pan and stir. Lower the heat and add the butter and parsley, stirring until the butter has melted and combined with the sauce.

Return the veal cutlets to the pan and coat them with the sauce. Transfer them to a serving plate and top with the remaining sauce. Garnish with lemon slices.

Poached PEACHES with Raspberry Sauce
Serves 4

T*his is the prettiest dessert—and always a showstopper!*

2 cups granulated sugar

2 cups water

4 peaches

1 pint raspberries

¼ cup confectioners' sugar

Vanilla ice cream, for serving

In a skillet, heat the granulated sugar and water over medium heat to dissolve the sugar. When it begins to boil, turn the heat to low and gently simmer.

Cut the peaches in half and remove the pits. If they are don't come out easily, you can remove them after poaching. Place the peach halves in the sugar syrup and cook until soft, about 3 minutes on each side.

Transfer the poached peaches to a plate, peel off their skins, and remove the pits, if necessary. Set aside to cool.

To make the raspberry sauce, puree the raspberries and confectioners' sugar in a blender or food processor until liquid. Strain the sauce through a fine-mesh strainer to remove the seeds.

To serve, place two peach halves on each plate, add a scoop of vanilla ice cream, and spoon the raspberry sauce on top.

Italian Wine

Enjoying a robust, full-bodied red wine with lasagna or pizza or a crisp, light white wine with fish or shellfish complements and amplifies the flavor of the food you have prepared. We rarely have dinner without a glass or two of wine, and our wine of choice is Italian. We believe that Italian wine is equal to any produced anywhere in the world.

Italians have been cultivating wine grapes for more than 2000 years. We love visiting the vineyards in Italy. Some of the vines are centuries old. So many excellent Italian wines are available, we want to give you an overview of the general categories. We could go on forever about the Italian wines we love. We advise you to experiment. Use the list that follows as a guideline for your selection.

MAJOR RED WINE GRAPES

Italy is well known for rich red wine. There are more than twenty types of red grape varietals in Italy. Let's take a look at some of the most important ones.

SANGIOVESE

This medium-bodied grape is planted throughout Italy, especially in Tuscany and Umbria. Sangiovese is the main grape of Chianti and Brunello di Montalcino. It is also used in the Super Tuscans. This grape has the flavor of cherries and herbs.

NEBBIOLO

This full-bodied grape makes two of Italy's most famous wines: Barolo and Barbaresco in Piedmont. These wines are among the best in the world.

LAMBRUSCO

This grape is used in the Emilia-Romagna region to produce a light, fizzy red wine of the same name.

BARBERA

Italy uses this dark-skinned grape, which is widely planted throughout, to produce wines with lower tannin and high acidity. Barbera grapes have an intense berry flavor. Since they are versatile with food, they are used in everyday table wines.

MONTEPULCIANO

This grape, grown in central and southern Italy, is used to make Montepulciano d'Abruzzo, a peppery, full-bodied, dark rustic wine. It is often confused with Vino Nobile di Montepulciano, a Sangiovese from Tuscany.

PRIMITIVO

This grape from Southern Italy makes a fruity wine that is similar to Zinfandel.

AMARONE

This Venetian wine is made with a blend of Corvina, Rondinella, and Molinara grapes. The grapes are partially dried, producing a richer, high-alcohol wine. This full-bodied wine pairs best with cheese or rich, savory foods.

VALPOLICELLA

Ripasso della Valpolicella is a Venetian style of wine made with Corvina, Rondinella, and Molinara grapes. The wine is produced by fermenting fresh juice with leftover pomace from Amarone winemaking. Pomace is the dark blackish-red debris—grape skins and stems—after the juice is poured off. Using the pomace makes the wine richer.

MAJOR WHITE WINE GRAPES

PINOT GRIGIO

The most familiar Italian white wine grape, grown primarily in northeastern Italy, is the Italian version of Pinot Gris. Pinot Grigio is dry and crisp, with the flavors of peach and a mineral quality.

GARGANEGA

This Venetian white wine grape is used in the regional wine called Soave. The wine is dry and crisp, with subtle fruit flavors. Soave Classico is sometimes similar in style to oaked Chardonnay.

CORTESE

This grape is used in the regional wine Cortese di Gavi from Piedmont. The wine is similar to Pinot Grigio or Chablis.

TREBBIANO

This is Italy's most planted white wine grape, which is also used to make Cognac and balsamic vinegar. Trebbiano is included in white wine blends all over Italy. In Umbria, it is called Orvieto. The grape produces crisp white wine that goes well with shellfish.

VERDICCHIO

This slightly bitter white wine grape is sometimes used in Soave, where it is called Trebbiano di Soave, which is not the same as Trebbiano. The wine is medium-bodied, crisp, and fresh.

VERMENTINO

This grape is grown in Sardinia and also cultivated in Tuscany. A Vermentino wine is a crisp white, often similar to Sauvignon Blanc.

MOSCATO

Moscato, cultivated in Piedmont, is best known for the sweet, bubbly Moscato d'Asti.

GLERA

This grape variety is grown mostly in northeastern Italy. It is used to make Prosecco, an aperitif. It is not always bubbly, but we like it that way. It is festive to start a party with the popping of corks! Who needs Champagne when so much great, affordable Prosecco is around?

Index

Note: Page numbers in *italics*
indicate photos of recipes.